COMMEMORATIVE CENTENNIAL EDITION

THE MAN FROM SNOWY RIVER
& OTHER VERSES

D0995223

AUSTRALIA'S BEST LOVED
POETRY COLLECTION

A.B.Paterson

INTRODUCED BY JONATHAN KING

Angus&Robertson
An imprint of HarperCollins*Publishers*

ACKNOWLEDGEMENTS

*Jonathan King wishes to thank Angus&Robertson for commissioning this centennial edition,
especially Angelo Loukakis and Clare Forster who managed the project; Jane O'Donnell and
Liz Seymour for editing and designing the book; the Mitchell Library, State Library of
New South Wales, Colin Beard (who supplied the photographs on pages vi, xiv, xvi, xxvii
and xlviii), Corryong Rotary Club and Jim Nicholas for permission to use photographs, and
Image Library services, especially Helen Benacek; Jane King for developing the project along with
Peter Blazey, Leslie Sprague, Roger and Angela Scales for inspiration; and the people of
Corryong who helped me to produce the 1995 centenary celebrations in honour of Paterson and
that elusive 'Man From Snowy River', whoever he may have been.*

DEDICATION
To my girls from Snowy River — Jane, Lowanna, Bryony, Mollie and Charlotte

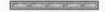

ANGUS&ROBERTSON
an imprint of HarperCollins*Publishers*

First published in Australia by Angus&Robertson Ltd in 1895
Centennial hardback edition 1995
This paperback edition 1996
Reprinted in 2000
by HarperCollins*Publishers* Pty Limited
ACN 009 913 517
A member of the HarperCollins*Publishers* (Australia) Pty Limited Group
http://www.harpercollins.com.au

HarperCollins*Publishers*
25 Ryde Road, Pymble, Sydney NSW 2073, Australia
31 View Road, Glenfield, Auckland 10, New Zealand
77–85 Fulham Palace Road, London W6 8JB, United Kingdom
Hazelton Lanes, 55 Avenue Road, Suite 2900, Toronto, Ontario, M5R 3L2
and 1995 Markham Road, Scarborough, Ontario, M1B 5M8, Canada
10 East 53rd Street, New York NY 10022, USA

National Library of Australia Cataloguing-in-Publication data:

Paterson, A. B. (Andrew Barton), 1864–1941.
The man from Snowy River and other verses/by A. B. 'Banjo' Paterson;
introduced by Jonathan King.
Commemorative centennial ed. (pbk.)
ISBN 0207 191735
I. Title.
A821.2

Designed by Seymour Designs
Front cover photograph: Stockmen setting off from a homestead on a muster,
A. B. 'Banjo' Paterson (from the 1895 edition)

Printed in Australia by Griffin Press Pty Ltd on 80gsm Econoprint

7 6 5 4 3 2   00 01 02 03

CONTENTS

INTRODUCTION ~ v

'The Man from Snowy River' ~ xxv

The Other Verses ~ xxxvii

FACSIMILE OF THE 1895 EDITION OF
The Man from Snowy River
and Other Verses ~ 1

CLASSIC TITLES FROM
ANGUS&ROBERTSON ~ 185

A. B. 'Banjo' Paterson, 1895

INTRODUCTION

To make any sort of job of it I had to create a character, to imagine a man who would ride better than anybody else and where would he come from except from the Snowy? And what sort of horse would he ride except a half-thoroughbred mountain pony.

A. B. PATERSON
The SYDNEY MAIL 21 DECEMBER 1938

This souvenir edition has been reproduced to commemorate the one hundredth anniversary of the first publication by Angus&Robertson of *The Man from Snowy River and Other Verses* by Andrew Barton Paterson — 'The Banjo'.

It contains exactly the same forty-six ballads selected by A. B. Paterson and George Robertson for the October 1895 edition. These were the ballads that produced Australia's first bestseller, creating a landmark in Australian publishing history. Paterson wrote most of the ballads before he turned thirty, in that first fruitful decade of his literary career — the golden years when he produced his best poetry.

In this commemorative edition we have tried to recapture the mood of that outback, pioneering, horse-drawn age by only

ACCESS TO THE MOUNTAINS IN PATERSON'S TIME WAS BY HORSE,
WHICH CARRIED SETTLER AND HOUSEHOLD GOODS ALIKE

using photographs from the period which Paterson, a very keen photographer, could easily have taken himself.

When Rolf Boldrewood introduced the first edition in 1895, he claimed that all true Australians would recognise that Paterson had 'touched the treasure-trove' which like 'undiscovered gold had awaited the fortunate adventurer' who had that 'somewhat rare combination of gifts and experiences' which 'the maker of folksong for our newborn nation requires'.

To understand the emerging bush culture, the writer had to be 'dowered with the poet's heart, he must yet have passed his "wander-jahre" amid the stern solitude of the Austral waste — must have ridden the race in the backblock township, guided the reckless stock-horse adown the mountain spur, and followed the night long moving, spectral-seeming herd in the droving days'. Having done that, Paterson had developed 'a finer sense which renders visible bright gleams of humour, pathos and romance'.

A pioneering settler related by marriage to the family of the third governor of New South Wales, Governor Philip Gidley King (of whom I am a descendant), Rolf Boldrewood, whose real name was Tom Browne, had already published the successful *Robbery Under Arms* in 1882-1883. And so against this background it must have been a great joy to Paterson to read Boldrewood's conclusion that 'in my opinion this collection comprises the best bush ballads written since the death of Lindsay Gordon'.

But the real significance of Paterson's verses was that they were the first truly Australian ballads. And this, despite the claim by Marcus Clarke in his earlier introduction to *The Poetical Works of Adam Lindsay Gordon*, that Gordon's verses were 'something like the very beginnings of a national school of Australian poetry'. Clarke himself was in a good position to assess new work, having already had *His Natural Life* serialised between 1870-1872.

But Paterson was a new phenomenon, no matter how much Gordon had previously written about horses and horseracing during the creative years following his arrival in Australia in 1853, until his death in 1870, when he shot himself. You could not smell the eucalyptus trees or hear the kookaburras in his poems the way you could in Paterson's. And Paterson was

THE UPPER REACHES OF THE
MIGHTY SNOWY RIVER

born in the Australian bush. Gordon, the son of an English army officer from Woolwich, migrated to the colonies as a grown man. His ballad 'How We Beat the Favourite' could easily have been written in England. But the stringy barks, the pine-clad ridges and the wombat holes not only place 'Snowy River' fair and square in Australia, but also 'up by Kosciusko's side'.

Paterson had already been publishing verses like 'Clancy of the Overflow' and 'Old Pardon, the Son of Reprieve' for five years, but with 'Snowy River', he confirmed his homegrown style and created a new Australian tradition. The genre was long overdue, and one hundred years into the new nation the Australian people welcomed it with open arms.

The book's success was soon greeted by the *London Literary Yearbook*. 'The immediate success of this book of bush ballads is without parallel in colonial literary annals, nor can any living English or American poet boast so wide a public, always excepting Mr Rudyard Kipling'. *The London Times* wrote, 'At his best he compares not unfavourably with the author of the *Barrack-Room Ballads*'. And from *The Athenaeum*, 'Swinging rattling ballads of ready humour, ready pathos and crowding adventure. Stirring and entertaining ballads about great rides, in which the lines gallop like the very hoofs of the horses'.

The first edition of *The Man from Snowy River and Other Verses* sold out in a fortnight. Three thousand copies sold in the first two months, six thousand copies within six months and ten thousand copies in the first year, all in a young country whose population was less than three million. Australia had its first bestseller. The book went on to sell over 100,000 copies and, as this centennial edition testifies, is still selling.

Books about Australia had sold well before, including both *For the Term of His Natural Life* and *Robbery Under Arms*, but no book of poetry — let alone Australian bush poetry — had ever been in such demand. It was obvious that George Robertson's publishing risk had paid off, as he confirmed in a letter to Paterson even as the book was being printed in October 1895. 'You will be glad to hear that Snowy River has beaten the record in Australian publishing…we intend to go on with a second edition at once. We expected that we would be required to go to press again this year, but did not calculate on having to do it before the publication of the first edition…such a thing has never happened in Australia we think.'

So Paterson, the unassuming part-time poet, woke up one morning and found himself famous. Overnight *The Man from Snowy River* became a runaway bestseller — the first bestseller ever written by an Australian about Australian subjects in an Australian idiom. Paterson became an icon, and soon was in great demand not only in literary circles, but also in the social world, where he was considered one of Sydney's most eligible bachelors. His aunt, Nora Clarina Murray-Prior, wrote to her daughter Meta Hobbs, 'All the world says that Bartie Paterson is engaged to a Miss Alice Cape a nice Roman Catholic, very

THE ELIGIBLE BACHELOR

musical, young lady but he has not said a word about it to his relations, and perhaps all the world is drawing conclusions from mistaken premises. Bartie has so many lady friends.'

When Paterson first submitted the verses in 1895, he had no idea what a success they would become. Having often published in *The Bulletin* under a 'nom de plume', he was nervous and uncertain about the first volume of verse that would appear under his own name.

The book was in fact inspired by *The Bulletin* editor, J. F. Archibald, who suggested to Paterson that he ask George Robertson of Angus&Robertson to publish a book of his best verse. Robertson agreed to publish the ballads if he could get enough quality material from Paterson by October, in time for the 1895 Christmas market. Paterson had just returned from outback Queensland, where he had recharged his bush batteries by visiting traditional sheep stations like Dagworth. While there he had also written words for a tune the station owner's sister, Christina Macpherson, had played to him, 'Thou Bonnie Wood of Craigielea'. Paterson called it 'Waltzing Matilda' and it went on to become the nation's most beloved folksong.

Returning to Sydney, Paterson agonised over the selection for his book, anxiously changing his mind right up to the last minute. George Robertson had already decided to start the collection off with such classics as 'The Man from Snowy River' and 'Clancy of the Overflow'. But in this first submission, Paterson only included eight other ballads (including his popular 1894 'Shearing at Castlereagh'), sending these to Robertson on 3 June. He did not know what else to select until Robertson hounded him for more material. So on 17 June he sent in another twenty ballads, including 'El Mahdi to the Australian Troops', the first poem he had ever published, written in 1885 to attack the sabre rattlers recruiting troops for the Sudan War. Robertson promptly rejected it as inappropriate for the collection.

For Robertson had a clear vision — he wanted to create a new genre of indigenous Australian verse. He therefore only accepted poems which fitted into this mould, and he sent so many of Paterson's verses back to the poet, that Paterson had to search hard to find enough Australian bush ballads that met Robertson's strict criteria. Eventually Paterson found more, including 'How the Favourite Beat Us'. But Robertson felt the book still fell short, so Paterson sent in a further selection, including 'Johnson's Antidote'. Robertson continued to reject and select from Paterson's submissions, until finally Paterson sent in eight more, including a number of last minute entries, such as 'Jim Carew' and 'Under the Shadow of Kiley's Hill'. George Robertson was finally happy. Angus&Robertson now had forty-six good quality ballads for the first book of truly Australian verse.

The entrepreneurial Robertson advertised the book widely, including an advertisement in Paterson's favourite outlet, *The Bulletin*. It was advertised under the heading 'Published This Day', and proclaimed it as 'Bound in Buckram and Printed on the best handmade paper, Gilt top'. It competed against another book advertised in the same display space, *The Devil in Sydney*, which tempted readers with bawdy tales of Barmaids, Baldheads and Mashers, along with a range of other titles including *The Ballet Girl*, *The*

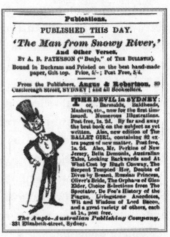

PATERSON'S BALLAD PROMISED
TO RAISE THE TONE OF THE DAY

Serpent Tempted Her and *Bella Demonia*, all offered by the Anglo-Australian Publishing Company.

Paterson's book was by no means the only contender for the discerning reader either, as it came in a rush of new publications, which included Rolf Boldrewood's *A Crooked Stick*, Louis Becke's *His Native Wife*, Mary Gaunt's *A Pointing Finger*, Ethel Turner's *The Family of Misrule* and Jim Hogan's *The Sister Dominions*. Despite this competition, *The Bulletin* reported that 'the greater part of the edition (1,000 copies) has been sold in advance'. According to *The Bulletin*, Paterson was ahead of his rival, Henry Lawson, who was also about to release a volumn of verse.

George Robertson distributed copies of *The Man from Snowy River* to booksellers thoughout the colonies, then sent out review copies to newspapers around Australia, and presentation copies to *The Times* in London, which compared Paterson with contemporary literary giants like Rudyard Kipling. Kipling, who enthusiastically reviewed *The Man from Snowy River* from an English point of view, was certainly excited by Paterson's discovery of a new Australian style. He also congratulated Paterson on his portrayal of a new Australian breed of man and called for Paterson to 'do it again', asking him to 'write more and more about the man who is born and bred on the land — without any moral reflections'.

Paterson's reassuringly traditional ballads were also popular during the mid 1890s because they provided a handrail of continuity for readers to hang onto during a period of dramatic political, social and economic change. When *The Man from Snowy River and Other Verses* was first published, *The Bulletin* and other newspapers were full of controversial issues dividing the emerging nation.

The outdated colonies were negotiating a new and threatening federal union to create the nation of Australia where the traditional powers of each colony would be undermined by those of the federation. The newspapers were full of the rights and wrongs of creating a federal government. The working classes were also challenging the upper classes, increasingly forming the first nationwide unions, organising crippling maritime and shearing strikes, and forming the Australian Labor Party. The maritime workers struck in 1890 and the miners struck in 1892, both crippling their respective industries. Then violent outback Queensland shearing strikes of 1891 and 1894 tore that state apart, as thousands of armed troops travelled to the back blocks and quelled the rebellion.

Shearers were killed and others placed in gaol for industrial insurrection. They were seen as martyrs, however and when they were released were greeted as heroes by a union movement that used them to win reforms and power.

Women challenged the old order even further, winning the vote in different colonies at different times, starting with South Australia in 1894. The worst drought on record, which lasted for ten years through the 1890s, sent thousands of farmers bankrupt and precipitated the worst financial crisis, bank crash and economic depression on record by 1893. Even the traditional world of the horse was being undermined by a series of new inventions including telephones, electricity, and bicycles. And, as if trains were not bad enough, a new form of horseless carriage was coming onto the market — the motor car. Even the theatres were full of strange new performances, with Sydney's Royal dominated by a long running clebration of Maori life — *The Land of the Moa*. Against this background, readers greeted Paterson's reassuring bush ballads about horsemen chasing wild horses on the high country with a sigh of relief.

MANY OF PATERSON'S READERS WERE HORSEMEN THEMSELVES

Unconcerned by these changes, Andrew Barton Paterson continued to promote the value of that age old animal, the horse. Born into a world of horses on Narrambla Station near Orange, New South Wales in 1864, Paterson's life spanned the passing of the horse. In some ways his work can be seen as a heartfelt eulogy to the demise of this wonderful creature he

HOMESTEAD WOMEN, LIKE THESE PENDERGASTS OF OMEO, TAUGHT
YOUNG COUNTRY BOYS LIKE PATERSON TO WRITE POETRY

had grown up with in the bush. His father, Andrew Bogle Paterson, had emigrated to Australia from Scotland, and had owned and managed properties for most of his life. His mother, whose parents emigrated to Australia from England in 1839, was born in the country herself. In addition to Andrew Barton Paterson, they had six children.

Having grown up during the height of the horse age on different properties in New South Wales, including 'Buckinbah', north of Orange until he was seven and then 'Illalong' in the central west until he left home, Paterson developed this passionate love for horses by riding them every day. When he began publishing verse, he even used the pen name of one of the family station horses, 'The Banjo'. He also learnt a great deal about the bush, catching yabbies in the creeks, shooting rabbits and helping muster sheep and cattle. So when he came to write bush ballads like 'Snowy River', he did so with great authority. As his parents lost property through drought and ended up managing rather than owning land, he also understood how tough life could be in the bush, even though he was later accused of romanticising this lifestyle.

Paterson was nevertheless a romantic poet, with an optimistic, high-spirited view of the world which he saw through rose-tinted glasses. He probably developed this romantic outlook reading Tennyson and Longfellow at Sydney Grammar School, which he attended from the ages of ten to seventeen, staying in Sydney during term time with his maternal grandmother, Emily Mary Barton, at Rockend Cottage, Gladesville. She taught him not only to appreciate but also to write poetry because she was a practising poet herself.

Some of Paterson's verses reflect something of her style, as can be seen in her poem 'Post Morning'.

And now we have come to the very last hill
But that is a steep one so Talbert, be still,
Walk gently to get yourself cool
When we get to the creek you shall have a good drink
If you'll only be good and stand quiet at the brink
And not wade through the mud till you're going to drink
Like a troublesome obstinate mule

But for Paterson, who studied law at Sydney University once he left school in 1880 and then joined a Sydney law firm, the bush was a romantic alternative to the city. Within a few years he was already complaining in his ballad 'Clancy of the Overflow' about the 'foetid air and gritty of the dusty dirty city through the open window floating its foulness over all'. He was also dreaming about the idyllic life of Clancy, as he complained further:

THE HORSE PROVED ITSELF AS A BEAST OF BURDEN IN PATERSON'S DAY,
EVEN TOWING STEAM ENGINES TO REMOTE MINES

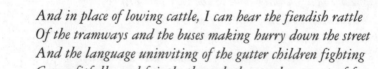

And in place of lowing cattle, I can hear the fiendish rattle
Of the tramways and the buses making hurry down the street
And the language uninviting of the gutter children fighting
Comes fitfully and faintly through the ceaseless tramp of feet
And the hurrying people daunt me and their pallid faces
haunt me
As they shoulder one another in their rush and nervous haste
With their eager eyes and greedy, and their stunted forms and
weedy,
For townsfolk have no time to grow, they have no time to waste.

These are very strong words. Paterson did not fabricate
these feelings. This was a highly personal autobiographical
condemnation of his compromised life in the city. His heart
was aching for the property he could never have and the

lifestyle he could never lead now that his father had gone bankrupt trying to beat the seasons.

Given his love for the bush and the creative spirit struggling to express itself, Paterson must have felt greatly constrained working in the city, as a lawyer of all things. In fact, he spent nearly fifteen years struggling to get free of that dingy little office and the cramping restrictions of the conservative legal world with its preoccupation with precedence.

But Paterson had been building up an alternative career for some years on the side. His first poem 'El Mahdi to the Australian Troops', the radical attack on the military leaders recruiting troops for the Sudan War, was published in *The Bulletin* in 1885. A string of ballads followed, including classics like 'Clancy of the Overflow' in 1889. Eventually by

PATERSON RODE WITH THE LIGHT HORSE DURING THE BOER WAR
AS A PRESS CORRESPONDENT

1899, after a series of literary successes, he cut the rope and freed himself, setting off for the Boer War as a Foreign Correspondent for the *Sydney Morning Herald* — an adventure from which he would never look back.

Paterson performed well at the Boer War, sending back interesting dispatches and participating enthusiastically in the conflict. He saw and reported a lot of action and even liberated Bloemfontein with a small party of journalists on horseback who arrived ahead of the allied troops. He also met and interviewed Kitchener, Churchill and Kipling, who became a lifelong friend.

Paterson returned to Australia and travelled around the country delivering lectures on the Boer War. In 1901 he sailed to China to cover the Boxer Rebellion, again for the *Sydney Morning Herald*. Although the fighting had stopped by the time he arrived, Paterson nevertheless sent back a series of stories on China and the aftermath of the rebellion, including interviews with the famous *Times* correspondent, Morrison of Peking.

Paterson then sailed to England, sending back a series of stories to Australian newspapers before returning to Sydney once again. In 1902 he decided to resign his legal practice, annoucing in his diary, 'Henceforth I am a journalist'. He then sailed to the New Hebrides to cover a new Australian colonisation scheme for the *Sydney Morning Herald* in the steamy jungles of present day Vanuatu.

On his return to Sydney in 1903 he was appointed editor of *The Evening News*. Later that year he married Alice Walker of Tenterfield and settled in Woollahra. The couple had two children, Grace in 1904 and Hugh in 1906. In 1908 Paterson resigned to go bush, buying 'Coodra', a largely unsuccessful property near Yass which he farmed until the outbreak of the First World War.

Having tried unsuccessfully to cover the war as a correspondent, Paterson enlisted as an ambulance driver in

France at Wimereux. He then enlisted in an Australian remount division and was commissioned a lieutenant in the AIF and posted to the Middle East, where he supervised the allied horses so successfully that he reached the rank of Major. His wife also served in a nearby hospital in Ismailia.

On his return in 1919, Paterson was appointed editor of *The Sydney Sportsman* and a horseracing contributor to the *Sydney Mail*. He retired in 1930 and devoted the rest of his life to writing books such as *The Animals Noah Forgot*. He was appointed Commander of the Order of the British Empire for his contributions to literature. He died in 1941 at seventy-six years of age.

Since his death, Paterson has been considered the literary giant of his era. His contemporary, Henry Lawson (1860–1922)

ALTHOUGH PATERSON SPENT SOME TIME RUNNING A COUNTRY PROPERTY,
HE RETURNED TO SYDNEY WHERE HE FOUND WRITING EASIER

shares that position, but to a lesser extent. The two were very different. Where Paterson was idealistic, Lawson was realistic. Lawson felt ambivalent about the bush. Paterson worshipped it. Unable to make a go of the bush, like his father, Paterson allowed Clancy to become his muse, his other self. So it was against this background that Paterson became an incurable romantic, yearning for the bush and a lifestyle he knew he could never have. Even when he tried running properties himself he failed and had to return to the city.

Lawson, who also grew up in the bush and had moved, like so many other Australians, to the city for economic reasons, criticised Paterson's idealistic view, because he knew how tough it could be in the bush. He had no hankering for that lifestyle and was happy to live and work in the city. In private correspondence he wrote that he had 'a horror of the bush' after abortive sorties into the outback, saying 'the bush between here and Bathurst is horrible. I was right Banjo wrong'.

For many years, these two leading Australian poets represented different social and political points of view. Lawson was an uneducated, working class, left-wing socialist fighting for reform, while Paterson was a well educated member of the establishment, trained as a lawyer — even if he had worked his own way up to that level. Paterson may have camped rough out in the bush on occasion, but this was through choice. Most times he went bush he travelled in coaches or on horseback. The penniless Lawson had no choice but to walk down at the level of the swagman.

Although the famous debate over the value of the bush, which the two poets held in the pages of *The Bulletin* in 1892, was pre-planned, there was nevertheless plenty of feeling in the poetic attacks from both sides. No matter who won in whose eyes, the debate established once and for all Lawson as the disgruntled realist and Paterson as the romantic idealist.

PATERSON COLLECTED MANY OF HIS STORIES FROM BUSH FOLK LIVING
IN THE COUNTRY, STRUGGLING TO MAKE ENDS MEET

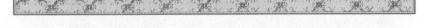

Paterson loved the eccentric bush characters so much that he created his own special world, the way Walt Disney created a magical fantasy world full of characters like Mickey Mouse. Paterson's world was full of fictional personalities like Clancy and Saltbush Bill. He then wrote about these characters so adoringly and with such a good natured sense of humour that he almost brought them to life.

By the time Angus&Robertson published *The Man from Snowy River*, Paterson had established himself as the leading bush poet, happily singing the praises of the Australian bush in a way *Bulletin* readers liked them sung. In the end, Clancy might have been Paterson's other muse, but as it turned out the romantic outback drover also became the favourite muse of an emerging Australia.

Despite the passing of time, Paterson still has the power to make a lasting impression on impressionable young readers. When my father gave me an early edition of *The Man from Snowy River* it changed my life, providing for the first time a purely Australian model with a complete set of values to guide me from then on. Whether later generations of young city slickers from many nations will be equally inspired only time can tell. But those new arrivals looking for cultural alternatives to the traditions they left behind will always find substance in the world created by Paterson.

For my part, I took one look at Clancy comparing his lifestyle with my dingy little office and promptly went droving outback where, in the 1960s, the western drovers still moved mobs of cattle along tracks like the dusty Diamantina. This was a pilgrimage that took me as a jackeroo into Paterson's world, where I mustered horses at the station mentioned in 'The All Right 'Un' — 'Wingadee' — and where I realised as I drove cattle through the area that there really was a town with the unlikely name 'Come By Chance'. It is against this bush background that I have written the introductions to Paterson's poems which follow.

The Man from Snowy River has certainly inspired a lot of spinoffs in the first hundred years since it was published. Over the century, Australian authors wrote scores of books on the topic, analysing the ballad and its significance for Australia. Australian painters, ranging from Broken Hill's Pro Hart to the Gold Coast's Robert Lovett, transferred the ballad to canvas, painting a series of scenes from the story.

Country singers like Sydney's Slim Dusty and Melbourne's Wallis and Matilda put the words to music, producing a range of records, audio cassettes and compact discs. By 1995 the Australian Bush Poets Association was also holding regular Australia-wide Banjo Paterson poetry readings, featuring 'The Man from Snowy River', while the town of Orange holds annual Banjo Paterson Festivals on the poet's birthday.

Film makers produced full length feature films in the 1980s by developing the story — *The Man from Snowy River 1* and *The Man from Snowy River 2*. These films sold so well internationally that a joint American/Australian television production company then produced a series in the 1990s for the world market, making the *The Man from Snowy River* a household name, not only in Australia but around the world. By the 1990s, the Americans were even organising *The Man from Snowy River* fan clubs and holding regular screenings of the film.

The Reserve Bank of Australia published a ten dollar note — soon nicknamed a Banjo — featuring Paterson's portrait and the opening words of the ballad in the mid 1990s. Behind Paterson's portrait were printed the words of the whole ballad in greatly reduced type in a panel which could be read when blown up to a much larger size.

ONLY HIGH COUNTRY HORSES COULD CATCH BRUMBIES ON KOSCIUSKO'S SIDE

Horseriding tourist operators conduct regular horserides in mountains up and down the Great Dividing Range, especially around Tom Groggin Station, 'down by Kosciusko's side'. Horsemen compete for the Cattleman's Cup with modern day heroes like Ken Connley claiming the title of 'The Modern Man from Snowy River'.

Little country towns around the Snowy Mountains have staked out claims as the centre of *The Man from Snowy River* country, including Jindabyne and Corryong.

Paterson could never have dreamed that the ballad he tossed off in an idle but inspired moment would ever be so celebrated on so many levels and in so many different forms. A modest and unassuming man, Paterson could never have predicted that within a matter of years the words with which he closed the great ballad itself would apply to the writer as well:

The Man from Snowy River is a household word today
And the stockmen tell the story of his ride

Although they have stood the test of time, Paterson was as hesitant about his ballads generally as he was about 'Snowy River'. Writing in a series of articles in the *Sydney Mail* in 1938 entitled 'Looking Backward', he said 'Our "ruined rhymes" are not likely to last long, but if there is any hope at all of survival it comes from the fact that such writers as Lawson and myself had the advantage of writing in a new country. In all museums throughout the world one may see plaster casts of the footprints of weird animals, footprints preserved for posterity, not because the animals were particularly good of their sort, but because they had the luck to walk on the lava while it was cooling. There is just a faint hope that something of the same sort may happen to us.'

THE MAN
FROM SNOWY RIVER

The best of the forty-six ballads, and the one focused on here, is undoubtedly 'The Man from Snowy River' — the ballad selected for the title of the original collection. A century after its publication, it has certainly become Australia's favourite poem. As Paterson predicted in the ballad itself, 'The Man from Snowy River' did indeed become a household name, not just 'down by Kosciusko's side' and 'around the overflow where the reedbeds sweep and sway', but in the classrooms, kitchens and even boardrooms of every Australian city and town.

Most Australians have heard of it and many of them take great pride in demonstrating how well they can recite it — especially when overseas. I first realised its importance outside Australia House in London in 1969. Returning from a working lunch, a female diplomat representing Australia stopped in her tracks and spontaneously recited it from start to finish! It has become an oath of allegiance, a badge of citizenship that Australians use to prove just how Australian they are. In over a quarter of a century commemorating historical anniversay events, I have never struck anything that inspires Australians more than 'The Man from Snowy River'.

Over the last century, this verse has become more than just another Australian ballad. In some ways it has grown to become Australia's equivalent to the old Arthurian legends, enshrouded not in the mists of time but in the mists of the Snowy Mountains. This uniquely Australian drama is set, not in Merlin's mythical Forest of Broceliande, but admidst the misty Kosciusko pine-clad ridges with their torn and rugged battlements on high. 'The Man from Snowy River' is our local version of King Arthur, leading his fellow knights into battle, not against a rogue dragon but a rogue stallion — the colt from Old Regret.

FEW BRUMBIES COULD ELUDE A TEAM OF AUSTRALIAN STOCKMEN,
WHO WERE AMONG THE WORLD'S BEST HORSEMEN

His loyal and constant companion, 'Clancy of the Overflow', reminds us of Sir Bedivere. Clancy stands by his friend to the last, just as Sir Bedivere did when he threw the sword Excalibur into the lake for the dying King Arthur. The fearless Harrison who 'would go wherever horse and man could go' doubles for the equally fearless Lancelot. These bush knights planned their campaigns, not at a round table but around mountain campfires. They chased wild brumbies that threatened valuable brood mares rather than mythical dragons threatening damsels. But their chase was just as difficult and their victory equally thrilling.

Paterson's ballad also builds on the ancient tradition of epic poetry. From the eighth century, epic verses like the European classic 'Beowulf' were used by illiterate tribes and clans to pass on legends from one generation to the next. In this light, 'The Man from Snowy River's' achievements can be seen as a variation of Beowulf's chase and then capture of the savage monster Grendel that had been threatening the Danish King.

The ballad itself is also one of the oldest forms of poetry, popularised by wandering European ministrels who sang their stories in medieval castles and village squares. It was the best medium for telling a dramatic story in verse, as the rhyming structure of the four line stanza made it easy to remember the story. This structure was used effectively by Samuel Taylor Coleridge, for example, in his 1798 classic, 'The Rime of the Ancient Mariner'.

Paterson also built on the tradition of Australian ballads, first brought to Australia by convicts and sailors, and used by bushrangers and their fans of later generations, such as 'The Wild Colonial Boy', with its defiant chorus:

We'll gallop over rivers, we'll gallop over plains
We'll scorn to live in slavery, bound down by iron chains

The dramatic story told by Paterson in his ballad is also based on the classic storytelling formula first used by Homer when he wrote about 'Ulysses', where the likeable hero has to win against impossible odds, even though others say he will never succeed. And 'The Man from Snowy River', like Homer's Ulysses, did achieve wonders. Paterson issued a challenge to this unlikely god of the mountains, sending him on an impossible mission against wild horses, which he passed with flying colours — 'till they halted cowed and beaten'.

But most of all Paterson really loved the Australian bush, and took his inspiration from its people and its animals — especially its stockhorses. So he wrote affectionately about all bushlife. This loving attitude showed Australians another side of the ordinary and harsh everyday world they took for granted — especially his promotion of the high country. In the 1890s, families who had

THESE LEGENDARY PENDERGAST BROTHERS WERE RIDING IN THE MOUNTAINS
WHEN PATERSON WROTE THE BALLAD

driven covered wagons over mountain walls and into hidden
valleys with their cattle in search of fresh pasture had a distinct
tribal culture of their own. Paterson recognised this in his
depiction of a special breed of mountain men epitomised by their
champion — 'The Man from Snowy River'.

Paterson thus created a romantic hero out of something that,
up to that point in time, had been considered ordinary. His
idealisation of Australian high-country horsemen gave the
young nation a new image. 'The Man from Snowy River' would
never be found in 'the old country' nor in the gun-toting wild
west of America — he was a uniqely Australian figure.

One of the main themes which can be found in much of
Paterson's work is the triumph of the underdog. Australians,
many of whom had started life as underdogs themselves, loved to
see one of their own beat a favourite. There were many more

convicts and their children per head of population in those days. From 1788 to 1868, when transportation stopped, four years after Paterson was born, some 166,000 convicts had arrived. There were also luckless gold diggers and thousands more who were out of work because of the great depression and drought of the 1890s. 'The Man from Snowy River' became a metaphor for a nation which may have started out as a convict colony but would one day, it was hoped, beat the world. Thus, in addition to a beautifully crafted ballad in the best heroic tradition, Paterson also produced a new Australian archetype — an ideal that could serve as a model for the growing and impressionable nation.

But Paterson's main passion was horses. He absolutely adored them, and many of his ballads sing the praises of horses he had come across in the bush or on the racetrack. In 'Snowy

ALTHOUGH PATERSON LOVED BUSH STOCKHORSES, HE WAS MOST PASSIONATE
ABOUT RACEHORSES, WHICH HE IDOLISED

River' he combines a wonderful horse with a wonderful horseman and forges a model that represents the best of both worlds. It is an influential model, still respected one hundred years later, not only by men and women from all walks of life, but by the high country horsemen it describes, who still cling passionately to an image which so clearly defines their identity. You can still see 'The Man from Snowy River' in the men who are chasing wild brumbies in the mountains today. For a young nation whose tradition is continually threatened by stronger forces as it drifts away from its rural roots, the model becomes more valuable as the years go by.

Most Australian reviewers agreed with Boldrewood's praise of 'The Man from Snowy River', writing favourable reviews. *The Bulletin* critic, A. G. Stephens, said 'the Banjo rides and wins his steeple chasing, and then sits down with a still

HIGH COUNTRY RIDERS STILL NEED THE SAME SKILLS TO MUSTER
AND YARD HORSES IN THE BUSH

tingling pulse and conveys the tingling to the pulse of the reader'. The ballad certainly honours that literary form. Beautifully structured with regular verses and eight line stanzas, it provides a rhyming pattern that is easy to remember and recite. The carefully selected words create an increasingly dramatic atmosphere by developing the plot through an increasingly racey metre that seems to reflect the rhythm of the rider himself, speeding up from walk, to trot, canter and then gallop. It is exciting to read and even more exciting to recite, and both the reader and listener gain the impression they are there on the great ride itself.

In December 1938, Paterson wrote in the *Sydney Mail* that he had written the ballad 'to describe the cleaning up of the wild horses in our own district, which was rough enough for most people, but not nearly as rough as they had it on the Snowy. To make any sort of a job of it I had to create a character, to imagine a man who could ride better than anyone else. And where would he come from except the Snowy. And what sort of horse should he ride except a half-thoroughbred mountain pony.'

'They have turned up from all the mountain districts — men who did exactly the same ride and could give you chapter and verse for every hill they descended and every creek they crossed. It was no small satisfaction to find that there really had been a Man From Snowy River — more than one of them.'

'The Man from Snowy River' himself was undoubtedly a composite character, based on different individuals Paterson had met. Like most writers he rolled different people into one character. These characteristics were based on real life because Paterson never wrote about anything he had not experienced firsthand.

The other characters in the ballad, like 'Clancy of the Overflow' and Harrison, were also composites based on a range of different characters he had met. Thus although some people

THE MIGHTY POWER OF MOUNTAIN STREAMS IMPRESSED EARLY SETTLERS,
WHO HIKED MILES TO MARVEL AT THE RIVERS THAT WATERED THEIR LAND

THE MAN FROM SNOWY RIVER & OTHER VERSES
PAGE XXXII

believe there is an Overflow which Paterson had in mind when he wrote the ballad, it was really a figment of his imagination. He had in fact placed the mythical Clancy, in the 1889 poem 'Clancy of the Overflow', 'droving down the Cooper where the Western drovers go' but if that was true, it would have taken Clancy a long time to ride over for the Snowy River chase.

Paterson also wrote the Snowy River ballad at about the same time he wrote a story based on his family property Illalong, called 'How Wild Horses Are Yarded'. So the poetic ballad could have been a flight of fancy from this account. They certainly rounded up wild brumbies at Illalong and one of the squatters in that district had a stud of Timor ponies that had escaped and joined the wild bush horses, producing offspring that were tough, fast, surefooted and could outrun any stockhorse. But having walked over the flat paddocks at Illalong myself, I can confirm Paterson's admission that it was not nearly as tough as the Snowy River mountain country.

Paterson could also have been influenced by similar ballads, including Walter Scott's 'Lochinvar', in which there was a rider who also had a good horse, and 'Through all the wide border his steed was the best'. Snowy River was certainly written in a similar style to Adam Lindsay Gordon's 'How We Beat the Favourite', which also sets the scene of the race, describes all the horses and riders present, identifies the favourite and the underdog, starts them off and then follows them to an exhausting finish — featuring a horse like Paterson's 'small and weedy beast'.

But none can outlast her, and few travel faster,
She strides in her work clean away from The Drag
You hold her and sit her she couldn't be fitter
Whenever you hit her she'll spring like a stag

Paterson's satirical verse 'How the Favourite Beat Us', which was included in this volume, also suggests he was aware of Gordon's poem.

Paterson's ballad had first appeared on 26 April 1890 in *The Bulletin*, unannounced and without any illustration on the page, apart from a cartoon ridiculing the education system. It followed a story about an eccentric New Zealand entrepreneur and was unceremoniously sandwiched between a series of advertisements for The Marvellous Optimus Watch, Horsford's Acid Phosphate (recommended by Physicians of all schools for the brain, nerves and stomach), Batho's Baking Powder, McDonald's Nail Trimmer and Scott's Emulsion of Cod Liver Oil with Hypophosphites.

This original version differed from the one published five years later by Angus&Robertson, and it is the later which has become the accepted version. Although Paterson made eight changes to the original, the most significant was transferring the location from 'down by Araluen where the stony ridges raise their torn and rugged battlements on high' to 'down by Kosciusko, where the pine-clad ridges raise their torn and rugged battlements on high'.

He also changed the starring horse from 'and one was there a stripling on a small and graceful beast' to 'and one was there a stripling on a small and weedy beast'. Otherwise, he only changed a number of words to improve the ballad. 'No better rider ever held the reins', for example, became 'No better horseman ever held the reins'.

Even though Paterson told the *Sydney Mail* that 'The Man from Snowy River' was not based on anyone in particular, a number of horseman have nevertheless been put forward in the hundred years since the ballad was written as 'The Man from Snowy River'. By the time of the centennial celebrations, there were at least seven contenders whose names had been registered.

Jack Riley of Corryong, who lived and worked on the Snowy High Plains property of Tom Groggin, was buried in 1914 as 'The Man from Snowy River'. His tombstone says 'In Memory of The Man from Snowy River' and was organised by veteran cattleman Jack Mitchell of Towong Hill in the 1970s. Jim Troy of Wagga Wagga was put forward by a Queensland stockman, Thomas Michael McNamara, who told the *Courier Mail* in 1938 that he was 'Clancy of the Overflow' and his younger brother-in-law Jim Troy was 'The Man from Snowy River'.

CORRYONG'S JACK RILEY

Owen Cummings of Dargo, who moved to the Northern Territory where he worked and died on Wave Hill Station, was buried with the inscription 'Respected as a horseman down Kosciusko way. The Territory's own Man from Snowy River'. The people of the Snowy Mountain town of Jindabyne claim it was 'Hellfire' Jack Clarke of Jindabyne. The people of Adaminaby claim it was Lachie Cochran of Adaminaby.

Historians have claimed it was James Spencer of Excelsior Station. Paterson visited Spencer when he lived at Waste Point on the junction of the Snowy and Thredbo rivers to interview him about his adventures guiding explorer Ferdinand von Mueller through the Snowy Mountains in the 1850s. And finally

CORRYONG. Coach off to Tallangatta 7.30 A.M.

WHEN HE WAS NOT RIDING HIS OWN HORSE, PATERSON TRAVELLED
AROUND THE BUSH BY COACH

Victoria's state historian, Dr Bernie Barrett, claimed in the 1990s it could have been an Aboriginal black tracker named Toby.

The legends about 'The Man' are based on several anecdotes like that told by the Mitchell family who own and operate Towong Hill Station near Corryong. They claim that when Paterson visited them in the late 1880s, old man Mitchell took him up into the mountains to Tom Groggin's Station, where he spent a night in an old slab hut drinking a bottle of whisky around the fireside with Jack Riley, who told him the story of the ride, and this inspired the ballad. There are many of these stories however, and most are based on unsubstantiated evidence. The fact that modern generations continue to search for the real 'Man From Snowy River' confirms the increasing importance of the legend to later generations of Australians.

THE OTHER VERSES

PRELUDE

Paterson wrote The Prelude in 1895 to introduce the forty-six verses. He was right when he said he had actually gathered the stories himself, for Paterson never wrote about anything he had not 'had a look at for himself'. He either experienced his stories firsthand or heard about them directly from somebody who had.

Paterson fashioned the 'fragments of song' in both 'earnest and jest' from 'rude stories one hears in sadness and mirth', because apart from generating respect for the bushman's life, he also wanted his readers to share the endearingly funnier side which he always saw.

PATERSON GATHERED MANY STORIES AROUND BUSH CAMPFIRES

OLD PARDON, SON OF REPRIEVE

This poem was first published in the 22 December 1888 issue of *The Bulletin*. On the 21 December 1938, Paterson reported in the *Sydney Mail* that this poem 'was an early effort founded on a family story. My father's cousin (known as Blenty because he wore spectacles, and "Blenty" is, I believe, Scotch for a man who wears spectacles) — my father's cousin anyway, owned a bush racehorse called Pardon in the days when they ran mile races in three heats.'

'Pardon was left in a stable at a bush pub on a very rigid diet, awaiting his race on the morrow, but being gifted with brains and resource Mr Pardon managed to knock down the rails of his stall and get at a bale of lucern. Tradition goes that by the time daylight came he had eaten most of it; but discounting this somewhat, we may assume that he had eaten

COUNTRY RACES WERE A GREAT SOCIAL OCCASION IN PATERSON'S DAY

as much as he could hold and he seemed in no shape for racing. In these circumstances his victory was, to say the least of it, creditable, and earned the tribute of a set of verses.'

Paterson also remembered attending a race meeting at Bogolong (now Bookham) when he was eight, with an Illalong rouseabout. They caught a jockey borrowing Paterson's light child's saddle to swap it with the heavier one off a horse called Pardon in the triple one mile race for the Bogolong Town Plate. The jockey told them to shut up, promising that if he won he would give the young Paterson a bottle of ginger beer. Paterson got his ginger beer and later said 'I worked the incident into a sort of a ballad called "Old Pardon, Son of Reprieve" '.

Although it is one of Paterson's longest ballads, the story is compelling enough to persuade the reader to see it through to the end, where as usual he is rewarded with an amusing twist.

Like Walt Disney, Paterson created his own special world of bush characters and animals who turned up from time to time in each other's poems and Pardon would turn up again in 'The Man from Snowy River' in the lines, 'There was Harrison, who made his pile when Pardon won the cup'.

CLANCY OF THE OVERFLOW

When this classic was published by the twenty-five year old poet in the 21 December 1889 issue of *The Bulletin*, Rolf Boldrewood greeted it as 'the best bush ballad since Gordon'. On 21 December 1938, Paterson wrote in the *Sydney Mail* that Clancy 'had its being from a lawyer's letter which I had to a write to a gentleman in the bush who had not paid his debts. I got an answer from a friend of his who wrote the exact words: "Clancy's gone to Queensland drovin' and we don't know where he are" '.

'So there it was — the idea, the suggestion of a drover's life, the metre, the exact words for a couple of lines of verse all delivered by Her Majesty's mail at a cost of a postage stamp.'

More than any other of his verses, 'Clancy of the Overflow' sums up Paterson's yearnings to live and work in the bush even though he was stuck in the city. The ballad also painted a wonderful picture of 'the sunlit plains extended' that idealised bush life imagery as never before. Although Clancy and the overflow were both fictional, the drover was also another character in Paterson's world who would reappear from time to time, especially in 'Snowy River' when 'Clancy of the Overflow came down to lend a hand'.

PATERSON IDEALISED DROVERS LIKE THE LEGENDARY
'CLANCY OF THE OVERFLOW'

CONROY'S GAP

Published in the 20 December 1890 issue of *The Bulletin*, this poem was based on a well known bush story which Paterson had heard. It was originally called 'The Story of Conroy's Gap' but Henry Lawson told George Robertson it was so well known that he should drop 'The Story of'. Paterson replied, 'All right. It suits me' and so it was dropped.

It is a classic story of a barmaid helping a bushranger already on the run, escape from the police. It is also a eulogy for a mighty horse, 'The Swagman' 'who could race through the scrub like a kangaroo'. It is one of Paterson's fastest moving and most exciting dramas — at its peak breathtaking. But it is also full of affectionate bush humour, complete with the usual rewarding twist at the end when the 'slinking hound' betrays both 'The Swagman' and his girl, Kate Carew, daughter of another of the characters who live in Paterson's wondeful world, Jim Carew.

The name Conroy crops up again years later in Paterson's 'Travelling Post Office', where some letters are sent care of Conroy's sheep. Like Clancy, Conroy, a knockabout bushman, was one of the characters in Paterson's wonderful world of the bush.

OUR NEW HORSE

This racing story was first published by Paterson, who was a keen jockey and punter, in the 22 March 1890 issue of *The Bulletin*. It is a typical Paterson portrait of a bush horse, 'Partner', whose owners sell it dishonestly only to buy it back again later by mistake. Although something of a moral tale it is nevertheless funny enough to make the reader laugh out loud as the inevitable concluding twist draws closer and closer.

AN IDYLL OF DANDALOO

The 1889 Christmas issue of *The Bulletin* contained this poem on one of Paterson's favourite subjects, country race meetings. This verse sings the praises of a small country hamlet that outwitted the city slicker who rode into town determined to take away all the prize money. Paterson always sided with the underdog, especialy when that underdog came from the bush. Dandaloo was the name of a New South Wales homestead to which the small hamlet was attatched.

THE GEEBUNG POLO CLUB

A humorous ballad which is pure Paterson at his satirical best, it first appeared in *The Antipodean* published by Chatto & Windus in association with George Robertson. Paterson, who was a keen and competent polo player, sets up a makebelieve city versus county polo game. It is an evenhanded attack on the 'irregular and rash' style of the country bumkins and the pomp and ceremony of Sydney's social polo club riders. As Paterson said himself, 'this polo business brought us in touch with the upper circles — a great change after the little bush school, the game-cocks and the days when I looked upon the sergeant of police as the greatest man in the world'.

Commenting on his life at the time, Paterson said 'Polo

THE CHAMPION POLO PLAYER

is another sport I'm very fond of, which accounts for "The Geebung Polo Club"'. The poem was inspired by a game he had played against a Cooma team, 'real wild men with cabbage tree hats and skin tight pants, their hats held on by straps under their noses'. He also believed in the military value of polo playing, saying 'no better training for riding, coolness and dash could be found for a young officer'. He certainly picked up the skills himself as his team won the 1892 New South Wales Polo Championship.

The action builds up throughout the drama and the imaginary slaughter of all the players on the field at the end is as total as the last act in Shakespeare's *Hamlet*. The outcome of this game has done little to deter modern polo clubs however, as they stage an annual re-enactment of the Geebung match in rural Victoria.

THE TRAVELLING POST OFFICE

Appearing in the 10 March 1894 issue of *The Bulletin*, this humourous verse explains how a father sent his drifting son a letter care of the mob of sheep he was droving. The poem picks up the theme used in 'Clancy of the Overflow' whose letter was 'for want of better knowledge, sent to where I met him down the Lachlan years ago'.

Paterson reported in the *Sydney Mail* on 21 December 1938 that he 'took the risk of describing how a letter was sent "Care of Conroy's sheep" ' rather than to any post office. I argued that they must sometimes send letters that way because the destination of travelling sheep is sometimes changed and a letter might lay unclaimed at a post office. Years afterwards I was travelling down the Diamantina on a coach. Across the waste of plain there came a dusty horseman to intercept us and as he rode up he said, "Have you got any letters on board for J. Riley care of the Carrandotta cattle?" and sure enough the driver had one.'

Paterson always seemed to spot the significance of these special features of the outback that were so different to life in the cities, and indeed in other nations, and preserved them for for posterity in his poetry.

'SALTBUSH BILL'

One of a series of three 'Saltbush Bill' ballads, this first appeared in the 15 December 1894 issue of *The Bulletin*. 'Saltbush Bill' asserted in these poems the native intelligence of the Australian bushman over the 'new chum' English jackaroo — a recurring theme in Paterson's work.

FEW WRITERS HAVE WRITTEN ABOUT LIFE ON COUNTRY PROPERTIES
WITH SUCH PATHOS AND HUMOUR AS PATERSON

In this poem, 'Saltbush Bill' distracts an English jackaroo, responsible for keeping sheep off his master's property, by staging a fight which goes on for a whole day. Although the Englishman thinks he is doing the right thing fighting off the bushman, Saltbush Bill is just filling in time so that his sheep can graze happily on the Englishman's land.

As Paterson said, tongue in cheek,

*Now the new chum fought for his honour's sake and the pride
of the English race
But the drover fought for his daily bread with a smile
on his bearded face.*

A MOUNTAIN STATION

First published in the 1891 Christmas edition of *The Bulletin*, this poem is a semi-autobiographical account of all the problems that ruined Paterson's parents. Having a property in the bush sounded idyllic, but once floods, droughts, dingoes and cattle rustlers struck, it was a different story.

Despite this prophetic poem warning city slickers of the dangers inherent in buying bush blocks, Paterson still wanted to get back on the land where he came from. He did in fact buy a property 'Coodra' (or 'Coodravale') some years after writing this verse. Ironically, he found it too difficult to make a go of it.

BEEN THERE BEFORE

Published with beautiful illustrations by Livingston Hopkins (Hop) in the 1891 Christmas issue of *The Bulletin*, this humorous ballad made fun of country townsfolk who tried to trick newcomers. Having worked on a sheep and cattle station

IN HIGH COUNTRY TOWNS LIKE OMEO, THERE WAS ALWAYS PLENTY OF
OPPORTUNITY FOR LOCALS TO PASS THE TIME OF DAY TOGETHER

myself, I can vouch for the dry sense of humour locals display
towards newcomers who they see as fair game for 'a bit of a lark'.

But in Paterson's poem the newcomer brings a stone with
him because he knows the trick, having been there before, and
thus outwits the locals.

THE MAN WHO WAS AWAY

A sad little poem first published in the 15 December 1894
issue of *The Bulletin*, it was based on stories Paterson heard
while working as a lawyer in Sydney. Country people were ill-
equipped to deal with the ways of business at the best of times,
but when a member of the family was also in gaol they did not
know how to handle it — except by saying 'he has gone away'.

As usual, Paterson takes the side of the bush underdog and is especially sympathetic in this case, remembering that his mother was also left to cope alone after the death of his father, who also had something of a problem with drink.

THE MAN FROM IRONBARK

One of Paterson's greatest classics, this popular ballad was first published with wonderful illustrations in the 17 December 1892 issue of *The Bulletin*. In telling the story of the clash of values between the bushman and city slickers, Paterson is dealing with a theme which fascinated him throughout his life.

By setting up the wandering bushman lost in the city on the one hand, and the flash barber and his 'gilded youths' in the shop on the other, Paterson propels both towards each other's throats. The ballad develops an inevitable momentum towards catastrophe, when 'The Man from Ironbark' believes the barber has cut his throat and resolves to get his own back before he dies.

THE OPEN STEEPLECHASE

Based on Paterson's own experiences of steeplechase racing, this ballad was first published in the 1891 Christmas issue of *The Bulletin*. Something of a champion himself, Paterson won the open steeplechase at the Rosehill Hunt Club meeting in 1896 five years after publishing this poem.

It is again the story of an underdog, the last-minute substitute jockey who is forced to ride on the horse 'Ace' against his will, but who wins the race after he is insulted by a rival jockey.

THE AMATEUR RIDER

First published in the 15 December 1894 issue of *The Bulletin*, this ballad drew on Paterson's own experiences as a jockey on the track. Written like a race call, the ballad tells the story of an underdog outsider jockey who — like 'The Man from Snowy River' — is given no chance of lasting the distance in a steeplechase race but who proves himself over the jumps. The outsider who was ostracised to begin with then becomes the darling of the track.

ON KILEY'S RUN

This poem, which was published in the 1890 Christmas issue of *The Bulletin*, was based on Paterson's personal experience in the bush.

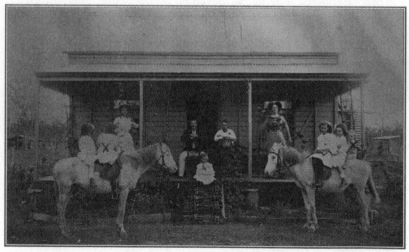

CHILDREN GREW UP ON HORSES IN PATERSON'S DAY, RIDING TO SCHOOL
FROM AN EARLY AGE

In his 1938 *Sydney Mail* reminiscences, Paterson said this was 'the story of a station or rather a lot of stations rolled into one. Bona fide settlers were referred to in speeches as the "sturdy yeomanry, the country's pride"; but in the course of time almost all them sold their blocks to station owners and moved on to fresh fields and pastures new — except that the station had become a vast freehold instead of a vast leasehold.

Paddocking came in instead of shepherding, the few remaining mobs of wild horses were run down and impounded and boundary riders took the place of the cattle hands. Thus passed this picturesque feature of Australian station life.'

FRYING PAN'S THEOLOGY

This short little exchange of dialogue between a country boy and an Aborigine, first published in the 16 December 1893 issue of *The Bulletin*, was based on Paterson's experiences growing up. His nanny was an Aboriginal woman called Fanny who taught him many Aboriginal stories, some of which worked their way into his poetry.

In the 1890s, white Australian often nicknamed Aboriginal people after everyday objects that they may have taken a liking to. In this case, the Aborigine was nicknamed Frying Pan.

THE TWO DEVINES

A song of praise for gun shearers, this poem was first published in the 15 December 1894 issue of *The Bulletin*. Paterson, who respected shearers who could notch up a decent tally, makes the point (tongue-in-cheek) that to be really dedicated, a shearer has to put his job before his family — even if someone is dying.

IN THE DROVING DAYS

One of Paterson's most moving poems, revealing his intense adoration of horses, it was first published in the 20 June 1891 issue of *The Bulletin*. As the poem confirms, he always believed a horse that worked hard should be rewarded. In this sentimental poem he romanticises the bush life of the drover as passionately as he did in 'Clancy of the Overflow' which was published two years earlier.

ONCE CAUGHT, BRUMBIES WERE BRANDED BY THE STATIONHANDS

LOST

This heart-rending lament was first published on 19 March 1887 in the *Sydney Mail*, when the poet was only twenty-three years old. In the poem, Paterson sees the death of the boy through the eyes of his own mother, who suffered many tragedies, including the early death of her husband. Paterson had seen children thrown from horses and killed while growing up in Illalong and this poem drew on those unhappy childhood memories. Young boys who went off on their own, sometimes without permission, to ride hard-mouthed, strong-headed horses always took a risk. The feelings Paterson evokes here from these memories made this an especially poignant poem.

OVER THE RANGE

This poem was first published on 26 February 1887 in the *Sydney Mail* and is something of a metaphorical discussion of life afterdeath, revealing a little about his early religious belief. He certainly inherited a Christian faith from his mother and grandmother who had gained great moral courage from their religious convictions.

In this poem Paterson confirms there is a heaven and that souls do meet again after death . To represent heaven he creates a bush metaphor, when he says the little bush child in this poem thinks people go 'over the range' when they die and meet others who died before them in the most beautiful country.

ONLY A JOCKEY

An early Paterson poem and only his fifth published work it first appeared in the 26 February 1887 issue of *The Bulletin*. Paterson had read in the daily press that 'Richard Bennison, a jockey, aged 14, while riding William Tell in his training, was thrown and killed. The horse is luckily uninjured.' A jockey himself at Randwick and Rosehill, Paterson was dismayed that the press report seemed to be more relieved that the horse was spared, than distressed about the poor boy dying. He worked his grief out through this eulogy to Bennison.

HOW M'GINNIS WENT MISSING

This poem was first published in *The Bulletin* on 21 September 1889 and is about an outback drinker, of whom there was no shortage in Paterson's bush days. The drinker, who just wandered off with a bottle and lay down by a river to sleep, was sadly taken away and drowned by the unpredictable and treacherous rising waters of the river. Paterson knew from his time in the bush that rivers could rise in an instant after rain and the worst place to sleep was beside one.

A VOICE FROM THE TOWN

An unusually sad lament from Paterson, first published in the 20 October 1894 issue of *The Bulletin*, this poem is about an old man who has let his youth pass him by. Like most of Paterson's poems, it was based on an incident from his own life during which he met an old character from the bush who felt he had wasted his life away working too hard. As such, it contains something of a warning from the adventure-loving and restless Banjo, who never let the grass grow under his own feet.

A BUNCH OF ROSES

This sad poem, first published in the 19 May 1894 issue of *The Bulletin*, shows the strength of Paterson's grief at the loss of a loved one. Although there is no evidence of any connection, he wrote it within a year or so of his mother dying. The long suffering Rose Isabella was only forty-eight when she died and Paterson organised for her to be buried with her family at St. Anne's churchyard.

BLACK SWANS

A lament for lost time that was inspired by a flock of black swans, this poem was first published on 22 July 1893 in the *Sydney Mail*. Paterson's reverie confirms the impossibility of going back in life to recapture things long gone. With its uncharacteristically maudlin mood and religious undertones, it reveals another side of the versatile author of 'The Man from Snowy River'.

THE ALL RIGHT 'UN

This endearing comment on the ill-fated schemes of a couple of outback wayward racehorse owners was first published in the 5 August 1893 issue of *The Bulletin*. Like 'Clancy of the Overflow' it romanticises life outback and once again refers to random letters from the bush, saying 'A letter came to hand, which read as follows'.

Having worked as a jackaroo myself on Wingadee, the station referred to in this poem where the bushmen were training 'Strife', I can vouch for the local enthusiasm for horses and the lengths people would go to to breed a winner on the country track.

THE BOSS
OF THE *ADMIRAL LYNCH*

An unusual foreign offering telling the tale of a South American hero, this poem was first published in the 10 December 1892 issue of *The Bulletin*. Although Paterson was much more interested in homegrown Australian stories, when he read about the bravery of the captain of a single gunboat, the *Admiral Lynch* standing up to an entire army, it inspired his respect for courage and he could not resist singing the praises of this bold underdog.

A BUSHMAN'S SONG

This song, which was first published in the 24 December 1892 issue of *The Bulletin*, actually became a popular tune in its time, and was often sung around campfires, in a manner true to our oral tradition. It has also been sung as a folksong like 'Waltzing Matilda'. Paterson probably picked up bits and pieces of this song and rearranged it for the bushmen who knew only too well the challenge of finding work along the track and the need to keep moving further outback.

PATERSON WAS ALWAYS INSPIRED BY THE RESILIENCE OF BUSHMEN WHO CARVED OUT A LIVING FOR THEMSELVES, TAKING THE ROUGH WITH THE SMOOTH

HOW GILBERT DIED

This poetic tribute to the life and times of the bushrangers
was published initially in the 2 June 1894 issue of *The
Bulletin*. Paterson had gone to school in Binelong with
descendants of Gilbert, the bushranger, so he knew and
understood the story of the bushranger's untimely death better
than most.

Paterson, a teenager when Ned Kelly was betrayed, caught
and hung, disapproved of any Australian bushman betraying
another, let alone handing them over to the police for cash.
Gilbert may have been outnumbered when he was trapped and
killed, but Paterson makes him a hero because he saved his
partner's life and greeted death full on and bravely.

THE FLYING GANG

Inspired by the outback railway gangs, this poem was first
published in the 18 July 1891 issue of *The Bulletin*. Paterson
was anxious to praise the railway workers who had done so
much to develop the bush. Even when he was a boy at Illalong,
the locals greeted the arrival of new railway lines with great
enthusiasm. But the real admiration was reserved for those who
worked around the clock — like the flying gangs.

SHEARING AT CASTLEREAGH

Paterson's shearing classic was first published in the 10
February 1894 issue of *The Bulletin*. Like the Tom Roberts
painting of the same period, *Shearing the Rams*, it captures the
atmosphere of the shed beautifully. It is another part of
Paterson's wonderful world of the bush, with the shearers

SHEARING WAS ONE OF THE GREAT 'PROFESSIONS' IN PATERSON'S DAY

coming from his favourite parts of Australia such as the Monaro to compete for the coverted title of the ringer (fastest shearer in the shed).

THE WIND'S MESSAGE

Published for the first time in the original 1895 edition of *The Man from Snowy River and Other Verses*, this poem harkens back to that 'Clancy of the Overflow' reverie of the city slicker wishing he was outback, where he belongs. Paterson criticises city people for not responding to the magical associations of the wind, which for him brings the fresh air of the bush into that 'foetid air and gritty of the dusty dirty city'.

JOHNSON'S ANTIDOTE

Now a popular ballad, 'Johnson's Antidote' was first published in the Australia Day 26 January 1895 issue of *The Bulletin*. Like 'The Man from Iron Bark' or 'The Geebung Polo Club', this humorous ballad paints a wonderful picture of the naive bushmen outback. Paterson loved the old bush characters and his endearing portrait of the ever hopeful Johnson was typical of his paternal feelings towards these humble people trying to make ends meet.

It is also a wonderful comment on the old Aboriginals who used to live on the fringes of white settlements, passing on only the traditional knowledge that suited them.

AMBITION AND ART

In this reflective and provocative poem which first appeared in the 26 May 1894 issue of *The Bulletin*, Paterson is confessing how much ambition rules the lives of artists and poets who become slaves to this at the expense of other values. He joins a long line of writers including Shakespeare, Dryden, Hesse and Goethe, who have claimed that the writer has to sell his soul to the cause. But Paterson coped with his muse better than most, managing to lead a balanced life despite the compulsion to write. He concludes that it is a worthwhile trade-off, because the love of Art is superior to the love of a woman as it is 'a star to guide thee' and the work of art 'lives for ever'.

THE DAYLIGHT IS DYING

This nostalgic verse was first published in *The Man from Snowy River* as a justification of the art of the poet and the singer. It is similar to Paterson's 'Prelude' and 'The Wind's Message', written the same year.

In the poem, Paterson explains how the attentive listener can hear all the old stories from the bush, passed on by the bird calls, the lowing cattle or the wind.

IN DEFENCE OF THE BUSH

As part of an ongoing debate Paterson was having with his contemporary bush poet, Henry Lawson, *The Bulletin* published this high spirited poem in the 23 July 1892 issue. This particular poem, which is reminiscent of 'Clancy of the Overflow', was written in reply to a poem from Lawson. Originally the first line read 'So you're back up from the country, Mister Lawson, where you went'.

OUTBACK TUG-OF-WAR

Compared to the city, Paterson claimed the bush was a wonderful world of beautiful sights and sounds peopled by noble pioneers. Lawson argued that Paterson was a myopic idealist who only saw through rose-tinted glasses. Lawson claimed the bush could be a terrible place where most souls scratched around desperately just to make a living.

The two poets planned the debate so they could put their

different feelings into verse, have fun and be paid for it. *Bulletin* editor, J. F. Archibald, supported them knowing the debate would help sell copies of his magazine. Although their feelings got out of control during the debate, the two ended up friends, with Paterson writing legal contracts free of charge for Lawson and looking after him in times of need.

LAST WEEK

A humorous poem first published in the 16 December 1893 issue of *The Bulletin*, 'Last Week' makes fun of people in small country towns who invariably say to visiting newcomers that they should have come last week when they would have seen all the things they hoped to see but did not.

Having grown up outside small towns like Binalong, Paterson understood that this traditional welcome was because the townsfolk were painfully aware of how little there was to show people from the cities. They are so short of real

HIGH COUNTRY STATIONS WERE LIKE SMALL VILLAGES IN PATERSON'S DAY —
EACH A LAW UNTO THEMSELVES

attractions in Binalong in fact, that when I visited the town to research this book, the building my first guide told me was Paterson's old school, turned out to be a private house.

THOSE NAMES

This poem was first published in the 20 September 1890 issue of *The Bulletin*. Paterson was always fascinated with names and used to spend hours pouring over maps and postal directories searching for interesting names for his poems. He loved both the Aboriginal names which he was taught as a child by his Aboriginal nanny, and those copied from England, and he worked them into his poetry wherever he could. In this case, he made up a poem just to celebrate the names, throwing in characters from some of his favourite places.

A BUSH CHRISTENING

Another Paterson classic, first published in the 16 December 1893 issue of *The Bulletin*, this is one of his most humourous ballads and, after 'The Man from Snowy River', one of the most often recited, both when it was originally published and today. Although it is not really autobiographical, Paterson himself was actually christened in the bush. He reported this incident in a family memoir years later, saying that his father and mother with their small son (known in the family as 'Barty') drove down across the mountains, stopping at Little Hartly for the christening of the child.

This youngster, like Maginnis Magee in the verses, had never before been in the hands of a 'Minister of Religion' and would have been equally nervous. Once again, the surprising twist at the end rewards the reader with a laugh.

HOW THE FAVOURITE BEAT US

This humorous poem was first published in the 9 November 1894 Rosehill racebook. A keen jockey, horse breeder, punter and racegoer, Paterson knew everything there was to know about race meetings. Having grown up in the period when Adam Lindsay Gordon wrote his classic 'How We Beat the Favourite', Paterson may well have written this as a tongue-in-cheek reply.

THE ANNUAL COUNTRY SHOW WAS ALWAYS A GOOD SOURCE OF STORIES FOR PATERSON, AS BUSH MEN AND WOMEN SWAPPED THEIR YARNS

THE GREAT CALAMITY

A light-hearted dig at the Scottish, this amusing poem was first published in the 19 August 1893 issue of *The Bulletin*. As he was part Scottish himself, Paterson had strong feelings for the Scots and this endearing joke about the

Scottish love of the whisky, complete with authentic dialect, is as close to the bone as any poet could get.

COME-BY-CHANCE

First published in the 21 March 1891 issue of *The Bulletin,* Paterson wrote this poem after stumbling across the name 'Come By Chance' in a postal guide. He did not know where it was. Having been sent there to round up some sheep myself when I was a jackaroo in the 1960s, I can vouch for the existence of this unlikely place. It is in the mid-north-west of New South Wales, north of Coonamble. While Paterson is actually right when he says 'there's really no such city' — 'Come By Chance' is nevertheless a nice little crossroads and in a good season a good grazing area.

UNDER THE SHADOW
OF KILEY'S HILL

Published for the first time in the original 1895 edition of *The Man from Snowy River and Other Verses,* this poem is a most uncharacteristic lament over an old bush homestead that has gone to rack and ruin, scattering its poverty-stricken family members. For once, Paterson sees and writes about the harsher side of the bush the way his realistic contemporary, Henry Lawson, often wrote.

As Paterson's parents had suffered bad seasons, went broke and fell sick at Illalong, this poem could have been written in part as an ode to their tragic times on the tough and unforgiving land. It certainly shows the poet was acutely aware of the darker side of bush life.

JIM CAREW

One of Paterson's recurring identities, Jim Carew, is immortalised in this verse, which was first published in the original 1895 edition of *The Man from Snowy River and Other Verses*. Carew also appears in 'Conroy's Gap', when his daughter Kate helps the bushranger Ryan escape. Paterson, who disliked heavy drinking himself, nevertheless sympathises with the former English gentleman, Jim Carew, who has fallen on hard times and resorted to the bottle — like so many of the characters in Paterson's bush world.

THE SWAGMAN'S REST

The last poem, selected by George Robertson for the 1895 book, was appropriately enough about the burial of one of Paterson's favourite characters — a swagman.

Paterson sympathetically tells the story of a drifter who lived 'a wasted life and hard, Of energies misapplied' who dies from the effects of drink. Like so many of Paterson's poems, it starts out on a simple note but ends up with a rewarding twist, this time with the unexpected discovery in the old swaggie's grave of 'a vein of quartz, all gleaming with yellow gold'.

It is like a pot of gold that the reader invariably finds at the end of the rainbow in Paterson's bush ballads — the best of which, like 'The Man from Snowy River', should still be in circulation in 2095.

BUSH CHARACTERS LIKE THIS TUMUT SWAGMAN LIVING IN HIS TREEHOUSE GAVE
PATERSON GREAT MATERIAL FOR HIS BALLADS

THE MAN FROM SNOWY RIVER

AND OTHER VERSES

A. B. Paterson

THE MAN FROM SNOWY RIVER AND OTHER VERSES BY A. B. PATERSON ("THE BANJO") WITH PREFACE BY ROLF BOLDREWOOD

LONDON

ANGUS AND ROBERTSON, LTD.

1913

Fifty-ninth Thousand

PREFACE

It is not so easy to write ballads descriptive of the bushland of Australia as on light consideration would appear. Reasonably good verse on the subject has been supplied in sufficient quantity. But the maker of folksongs for our newborn nation requires a somewhat rare combination of gifts and experiences. Dowered with the poet's heart, he must yet have passed his ' wander-jähre ' amid the stern solitude of the Austral waste—must have ridden the race in the back-block township, guided the reckless stock-horse adown the mountain spur, and followed the night-long moving, spectral-seeming herd ' in the droving days.' Amid such scarce congenial surroundings comes oft that finer sense which renders visible bright gleams of humour, pathos, and romance, which, like undiscovered gold, await the fortunate adventurer. That the author has touched this treasure-trove, not less delicately than distinctly, no true Australian will deny. In my opinion this collection comprises the best bush ballads written since the death of Lindsay Gordon.

ROLF BOLDREWOOD

A number of these verses are now published for the first time, most of the others were written for and appeared in "The Bulletin" (Sydney, N.S.W.), and are therefore already widely known to readers in Australasia.

A. B. PATERSON

PRELUDE

I have gathered these stories afar,
  In the wind and the rain,
In the land where the cattle camps are,
  On the edge of the plain.
On the overland routes of the west,
  When the watches were long,
I have fashioned in earnest and jest
  These fragments of song.

They are just the rude stories one hears
  In sadness and mirth,
The records of wandering years,
  And scant is their worth
Though their merits indeed are but slight,
  I shall not repine,
If they give you one moment's delight,
  Old comrades of mine.

CONTENTS

PAGE

PRELUDE
I have gathered these stories afar, - - ix

THE MAN FROM SNOWY RIVER
There was movement at the station, for
the word had passed around - - 3

OLD PARDON, THE SON OF REPRIEVE
You never heard tell of the story ? - 10

CLANCY OF THE OVERFLOW
I had written him a letter which I had,
for want of better, - - - 20

CONROY'S GAP
This was the way of it, don't you know— 23

OUR NEW HORSE
The boys had come back from the races - 31

CONTENTS

AN IDYLL OF DANDALOO   PAGE
    On Western plains, where shade is not, -   38

THE GEEBUNG POLO CLUB
    It was somewhere up the country, in a
    land of rock and scrub—   -   -   -   43

THE TRAVELLING POST OFFICE
    The roving breezes come and go, the reed
    beds sweep and sway, -   -   -   -   47

SALTBUSH BILL
    Now this is the law of the Overland that
    all in the West obey.   -   -   -   50

A MOUNTAIN STATION
    I bought a run a while ago,   -   -   -   56

BEEN THERE BEFORE
    There came a stranger to Walgett town -   59

THE MAN WHO WAS AWAY
    The widow sought the lawyer's room with
    children three in tow   -   -   -   -   61

THE MAN FROM IRONBARK
    It was the man from Ironbark who struck
    the Sydney town, -   -   -   -   -   64

PAGE

THE OPEN STEEPLECHASE

    I had ridden over hurdles up the country

        once or twice, - - - - -   69

THE AMATEUR RIDER

    Him going to ride for us! *Him*—with the

        pants and the eyeglass and all - -   75

ON KILEY'S RUN

    The roving breezes come and go   - -   80

FRYINGPAN'S THEOLOGY

    Scene : On Monaro. -   -   - - -   86

THE TWO DEVINES

    It was shearing-time at the Myall Lake, -   88

IN THE DROVING DAYS

    'Only a pound,' said the auctioneer,   -   91

LOST

    'He ought to be home,' said the old man,

        without there's something amiss. - -   96

OVER THE RANGE

    Little bush-maiden, wondering-eyed,   - 100

PAGE

ONLY A JOCKEY

Out in the grey cheerless chill of the
morning light, ... 102

HOW McGINNIS WENT MISSING

Let us cease our idle chatter, . . . 105

A VOICE FROM THE TOWN

I thought, in the days of the droving, . 107

A BUNCH OF ROSES

Roses ruddy and roses white, . . . 111

BLACK SWANS

As I lie at rest on a patch of clover . 113

THE ALL RIGHT 'UN

He came from 'further out,' . . . 117

THE BOSS OF THE ADMIRAL LYNCH

Did you ever hear tell of Chili? I was
readin' the other day 120

A BUSHMAN'S SONG

I'm travelling down the Castlereagh, and
I'm a station hand, ... 125

HOW GILBERT DIED

There's never a stone at the sleeper's head, 129

CONTENTS

PAGE

THE FLYING GANG
I served my time, in the days gone by,　134

SHEARING AT CASTLEREAGH
The bell is set aringing, and the engine
gives a toot,　.　.　.　.　.　136

THE WIND'S MESSAGE
There came a whisper down the Bland
between the dawn and dark,　.　.　139

JOHNSON'S ANTIDOTE
Down along the Snakebite River, where
the overlanders camp,　.　.　142

AMBITION AND ART
I am the maid of the lustrous eyes .　.　149

THE DAYLIGHT IS DYING
The daylight is dying　.　.　.　.　153

IN DEFENCE OF THE BUSH
So you're back from up the country,
Mister Townsman, where you went,　.　156

LAST WEEK
Oh, the new-chum went to the back block
run,　.　.　.　.　.　.　.　160

xvi CONTENTS

THOSE NAMES
The shearers sat in the firelight, hearty
and hale and strong, - - - - 162

A BUSH CHRISTENING
On the outer Barcoo where the churches
are few, - - - - - - - 165

HOW THE FAVOURITE BEAT US
'Aye,' said the boozer, ' I tell you it's
true, sir, - - - - - - 168

THE GREAT CALAMITY
MacFierce'un came to Whiskeyhurst - 171

COME-BY-CHANCE
As I pondered very weary o'er a volume
long and dreary— - - - - 174

UNDER THE SHADOW OF KILEY'S HILL
This is the place where they all were bred ; 177

JIM CAREW
Born of a thoroughbred English race, - 179

THE SWAGMEN'S REST
We buried old Bob where the bloodwoods
wave - - - - - - - 182

THE MAN FROM SNOWY RIVER

AND OTHER VERSES

THE MAN FROM SNOWY RIVER.

THERE was movement at the station, for the word had
    passed around
That the colt from old Regret had got away,
And had joined the wild bush horses—he was worth
    a thousand pound,
So all the cracks had gathered to the fray.
All the tried and noted riders from the stations near
    and far
Had mustered at the homestead overnight,
For the bushmen love hard riding where the wild
    bush horses are,
And the stock-horse snuffs the battle with delight.

There was Harrison, who made his pile when
    Pardon won the cup,
The old man with his hair as white as snow ;
But few could ride beside him when his blood was
    fairly up—
He would go wherever horse and man could go.

And Clancy of the Overflow came down to lend a
      hand,
   No better horseman ever held the reins ;
For never horse could throw him while the saddle-
      girths would stand,
   He learnt to ride while droving on the plains.

And one was there, a stripling on a small and weedy
      beast,
   He was something like a racehorse undersized,
With a touch of Timor pony—three parts thorough-
      bred at least—
   And such as are by mountain horsemen prized.
He was hard and tough and wiry—just the sort that
      won't say die—
   There was courage in his quick impatient tread ;
And he bore the badge of gameness in his bright and
      fiery eye,
   And the proud and lofty carriage of his head.

But still so slight and weedy, one would doubt his
      power to stay,
   And the old man said, 'That horse will never do
For a long and tiring gallop—lad, you'd better stop
   away,

'Those hills are far too rough for such as you.'
So he waited sad and wistful—only Clancy stood his
    friend—
  'I think we ought to let him come,' he said ;
'I warrant he'll be with us when he's wanted at the
    end,
  'For both his horse and he are mountain bred.

'He hails from Snowy River, up by Kosciusko's side,
  'Where the hills are twice as steep and twice as
    rough,
'Where a horse's hoofs strike firelight from the flint
    stones every stride,
  'The man that holds his own is good enough.
'And the Snowy River riders on the mountains make
    their home,
  'Where the river runs those giant hills between ;
'I have seen full many horsemen since I first com-
    menced to roam,
  'But nowhere yet such horsemen have I seen.'

So he went—they found the horses by the big mimosa
    clump—
They raced away towards the mountain's brow,

And the old man gave his orders, ' Boys, go at them
   from the jump,
  ' No use to try for fancy riding now.
  And, Clancy, you must wheel them, try and wheel
   them to the right.
  ' Ride boldly, lad, and never fear the spills,
' For never yet was rider that could keep the mob in
   sight,
  ' If once they gain the shelter of those hills.'

So Clancy rode to wheel them—he was racing on the
   wing
  Where the best and boldest riders take their place,
And he raced his stock-horse past them, and he made
   the ranges ring
  With the stockwhip, as he met them face to face.
Then they halted for a moment, while he swung the
   dreaded lash,
  But they saw their well-loved mountain full in view,
And they charged beneath the stockwhip with a
   sharp and sudden dash,
  And off into the mountain scrub they flew.

Then fast the horsemen followed, where the gorges
   deep and black

Resounded to the thunder of their tread,
And the stockwhips woke the echoes, and they fiercely
 answered back
From cliffs and crags that beetled overhead.
And upward, ever upward, the wild horses held their
 way,
 Where mountain ash and kurrajong grew wide ;
And the old man muttered fiercely, ' We may bid the
 mob good day,
 ' *No* man can hold them down the other side.'

When they reached the mountain's summit, even
 Clancy took a pull,
 It well might make the boldest hold their breath,
The wild hop scrub grew thickly, and the hidden
 ground was full
 Of wombat holes, and any slip was death.
But the man from Snowy River let the pony have his
 head,
 And he swung his stockwhip round and gave a
 cheer,
And he raced him down the mountain like a torrent
 down its bed,
 While the others stood and watched in very fear.

He sent the flint stones flying, but the pony kept his
　　feet,
　He cleared the fallen timber in his stride,
And the man from Snowy River never shifted in his
　　seat—
　It was grand to see that mountain horseman ride.
Through the stringy barks and saplings, on the rough
　　and broken ground,
　Down the hillside at a racing pace he went ;
And he never drew the bridle till he landed safe and
　　sound,
　At the bottom of that terrible descent.

He was right among the horses as they climbed the
　　further hill,
　And the watchers on the mountain standing mute,
Saw him ply the stockwhip fiercely, he was right
　　among them still,
　As he raced across the clearing in pursuit.
Then they lost him for a moment, where two moun-
　　tain gullies met
　In the ranges, but a final glimpse reveals
On a dim and distant hillside the wild horses racing
　　yet,
　With the man from Snowy River at their heels.

And he ran them single-handed till their sides were
    white with foam.
He followed like a bloodhound on their track,
Till they halted cowed and beaten, then he turned
    their heads for home,
And alone and unassisted brought them back.
But his hardy mountain pony he could scarcely raise
    a trot,
He was blood from hip to shoulder from the spur ;
But his pluck was still undaunted, and his courage
    fiery hot,
For never yet was mountain horse a cur.

And down by Kosciusko, where the pine-clad ridges
    raise
Their torn and rugged battlements on high,
Where the air is clear as crystal, and the white
    stars fairly blaze
At midnight in the cold and frosty sky,
And where around the Overflow the reedbeds sweep
    and sway
To the breezes, and the rolling plains are wide,
The man from Snowy River is a household word
    to-day,
And the stockmen tell the story of his ride.

OLD PARDON THE SON OF REPRIEVE.

You never heard tell of the story ?
    Well, now, I can hardly believe !
Never heard of the honour and glory
    Of Pardon, the son of Reprieve ?
But maybe you're only a Johnnie
    And don't know a horse from a hoe ?
Well, well, don't get angry, my sonny,
    But, really, a young un should know.

They bred him out back on the 'Never,'
    His mother was Mameluke breed.
To the front—and then stay there—was ever
    The root of the Mameluke creed.
He seemed to inherit their wiry
    Strong frames—and their pluck to receive—
As hard as a flint and as fiery
    Was Pardon, the son of Reprieve.
10

We ran him at many a meeting
   At crossing and gully and town,
And nothing could give him a beating—
   At least when our money was down.
For weight wouldn't stop him, nor distance,
   Nor odds, though the others were fast,
He'd race with a dogged persistence,
   And wear them all down at the last.

At the Turon the Yattendon filly
   Led by lengths at the mile-and-a-half,
And we all began to look silly,
   While *her* crowd were starting to laugh ;
But the old horse came faster and faster,
   His pluck told its tale, and his strength,
He gained on her, caught her, and passed her,
   And won it, hands-down, by a length.

And then we swooped down on Menindie
   To run for the President's Cup—
Oh ! that's a sweet township—a shindy
   To them is board, lodging, and sup.
Eye-openers they are, and their system
   Is never to suffer defeat ;

It's ' win, tie, or wrangle '—to best 'em
     You must lose 'em, or else it's ' dead heat.'

We strolled down the township and found 'em
     At drinking and gaming and play ;
If sorrows they had, why they drowned 'em,
     And betting was soon under way.
Their horses were good 'uns and fit 'uns,
     There was plenty of cash in the town ;
They backed their own horses like Britons,
     And, Lord ! how *we* rattled it down !

With gladness we thought of the morrow,
     We counted our wagers with glee,
A simile homely to borrow—
     ' There was plenty of milk in our tea.'
You see we were green ; and we never
     Had even a thought of foul play,
Though we well might have known that the clever
     Division would ' put us away.'

Experience ' *docet*,' they tell us,
     At least so I've frequently heard,
But, ' dosing ' or ' stuffing,' those fellows
     Were up to each move on the board ;

They got to his stall—it is sinful
  To think what such villains would do—
And they gave him a regular skinful
  Of barley—green barley—to chew.

He munched it all night, and we found him
  Next morning as full as a hog—
The girths wouldn't nearly meet round him ;
  He looked like an overfed frog.
We saw we were done like a dinner—
  The odds were a thousand to one
Against Pardon turning up winner,
  'Twas cruel to ask him to run.

We got to the course with our troubles,
  A crestfallen couple were we ;
And we heard the ' books ' calling the doubles—
  A roar like the surf of the sea ;
And over the tumult and louder
  Rang ' Any price Pardon, I lay ! '
Says Jimmy, ' The children of Judah
  ' Are out on the warpath to-day

Three miles in three heats :—Ah, my sonny,
    The horses in those days were stout,
They had to run well to win money ;
    I don't see such horses about.
Your six-furlong vermin that scamper
    Half-a-mile with their feather-weight up ;
They wouldn't earn much of their damper
    In a race like the President's Cup.

The first heat was soon set a-going ;
    The Dancer went off to the front ;
The Don on his quarters was showing,
    With Pardon right out of the hunt.
He rolled and he weltered and wallowed—
    You'd kick your hat faster, I'll bet ;
They finished all bunched, and he followed
    All lathered and dripping with sweat.

But troubles came thicker upon us,
    For while we were rubbing him dry
The stewards came over to warn us :
    ' We hear you are running a bye !
If Pardon don't spiel like tarnation
    ' And win the next heat—if he can—

'He'll earn a disqualification;
   'Just think over *that*, now, my man!'

Our money all gone and our credit,
   Our horse couldn't gallop a yard;
And then people thought that *we* did it!
   It really was terribly hard.
We were objects of mirth and derision
   To folk in the lawn and the stand,
And the yells of the clever division
   Of 'Any price Pardon!' were grand.

We still had a chance for the money,
   Two heats still remained to be run;
If both fell to us—why, my sonny,
   The clever division were done.
And Pardon was better, we reckoned,
   His sickness was passing away,
So he went to the post for the second
   And principal heat of the day.

They're off and away with a rattle,
   Like dogs from the leashes let slip,
And right at the back of the battle
   He followed them under the whip.

They gained ten good lengths on him quickly
    He dropped right away from the pack;
I tell you it made me feel sickly
    To see the blue jacket fall back.

Our very last hope had departed—
    We thought the old fellow was done,
When all of a sudden he started
    To go like a shot from a gun.
His chances seemed slight to embolden
    Our hearts; but, with teeth firmly set,
We thought, 'Now or never! The old 'un
    ' May reckon with some of 'em yet.'

Then loud rose the war-cry for Pardon;
    He swept like the wind down the dip,
And over the rise by the garden,
    The jockey was done with the whip
The field were at sixes and sevens—
    The pace at the first had been fast—
And hope seemed to drop from the heavens,
    For Pardon was coming at last.

And how he did come! It was splendid;
    He gained on them yards every bound,

Stretching out like a greyhound extended,
  His girth laid right down on the ground.
A shimmer of silk in the cedars
  As into the running they wheeled,
And out flashed the whips on the leaders,
  For Pardon had collared the field.

Then right through the ruck he came sailing—
  I knew that the battle was won—
The son of Haphazard was failing,
  The Yattendon filly was done ;
He cut down the Don and the Dancer,
  He raced clean away from the mare—
He's in front !   Catch him now if you can, sir !
  And up went my hat in the air !

Then loud from the lawn and the garden
  Rose offers of ' Ten to one *on* ! '
' Who'll bet on the field ?   I back Pardon !'
  No use ; all the money was gone.
He came for the third heat light-hearted,
  A-jumping and dancing about ;
The others were done ere they started
  Crestfallen, and tired, and worn out.

B

He won it, and ran it much faster
  Than even the first, I believe
Oh, he was the daddy, the master,
  Was Pardon, the son of Reprieve.
He showed 'em the method to travel—
  The boy sat as still as a stone—
They never could see him for gravel;
  He came in hard-held, and alone.

.   .   .   .   .   .

But he's old—and his eyes are grown hollow
  Like me, with my thatch of the snow;
When he dies, then I hope I may follow,
  And go where the racehorses go.
I don't want no harping nor singing—
  Such things with my style don't agree;
Where the hoofs of the horses are ringing
  There's music sufficient for me.

And surely the thoroughbred horses
  Will rise up again and begin
Fresh races on far-away courses,
  And p'raps they might let me slip in

It would look rather well the race-card on
   'Mongst Cherubs and Seraphs and things,
' Angel Harrison's black gelding Pardon,
   ' Blue halo, white body and wings.'

And if they have racing hereafter,
   (And who is to say they will not ?)
When the cheers and the shouting and laughter
   Proclaim that the battle grows hot ;
As they come down the racecourse a-steering,
   He'll rush to the front, I believe ;
And you'll hear the great multitude cheering
   For Pardon, the son of Reprieve.

CLANCY OF THE OVERFLOW

I HAD written him a letter which I had, for want of
    better
    Knowledge, sent to where I met him down the
      Lachlan, years ago,
He was shearing when I knew him, so I sent the
    letter to him,
    Just 'on spec,' addressed as follows, 'Clancy, of
      The Overflow.'

And an answer came directed in a writing unex-
    pected,
    (And I think the same was written with a
      thumb-nail dipped in tar)
'Twas his shearing mate who wrote it, and *verbatim*
    I will quote it :
    'Clancy's gone to Queensland droving, and we
      don't know where he are.

.   .   .   .   .   .

In my wild erratic fancy visions come to me of Clancy
   Gone a-droving 'down the Cooper' where the
      Western drovers go ;
As the stock are slowly stringing, Clancy rides be-
   hind them singing,
   For the drover's life has pleasures that the towns-
      folk never know.

And the bush hath friends to meet him, and their
      kindly voices greet him
   In the murmur of the breezes and the river on its
      bars,
And he sees the vision splendid of the sunlit plains
      extended,
   And at night the wond'rous glory of the everlasting
      stars.

    .   .   .   .   .   .

I am sitting in my dingy little office, where a stingy
   Ray of sunlight struggles feebly down between the
      houses tall,
And the fœtid air and gritty of the dusty, dirty city
   Through the open window floating spreads its
      foulness over all

And in place of lowing cattle, I can hear the fiendish
    rattle
    Of the tramways and the 'buses making hurry
    down the street,
And the language uninviting of the gutter children
    fighting,
    Comes fitfully and faintly through the ceaseless
    tramp of feet.

And the hurrying people daunt me, and their pallid
    faces haunt me
    As they shoulder one another in their rush and
    nervous haste,
With their eager eyes and greedy, and their stunted
    forms and weedy,
    For townsfolk have no time to grow, they have no
    time to waste.

And I somehow rather fancy that I'd like to change
    with Clancy,
    Like to take a turn at droving where the seasons
    come and go,
While he faced the round eternal of the cash-book
    and the journal—
    But I doubt he'd suit the office, Clancy, of ' The
    Overflow.'

CONROY'S GAP

THIS was the way of it, don't you know—
　　Ryan was 'wanted' for stealing sheep,
And never a trooper, high or low,
　　Could find him—catch a weasel asleep!
Till Trooper Scott, from the Stockman's Ford—
　　A bushman, too, as I've heard them tell—
Chanced to find him drunk as a lord
　　Round at the Shadow of Death Hotel.

D' you know the place？　It's a wayside inn,
　　A low grog-shanty—a bushman trap,
Hiding away in its shame and sin
　　Under the shelter of Conroy's Gap—
Under the shade of that frowning range,
　　The roughest crowd that ever drew breath—
Thieves and rowdies, uncouth and strange,
　　Were mustered round at the Shadow of Death.

23

The trooper knew that his man would slide
  Like a dingo pup, if he saw the chance :
And with half a start on the mountain side
  Ryan would lead him a merry dance.
Drunk as he was when the trooper came,
  To him that did not matter a rap—
Drunk or sober, he was the same,
  The boldest rider in Conroy's Gap.

' I want you, Ryan,' the trooper said,
  ' And listen to me, if you dare resist,
' So help me heaven, I'll shoot you dead ! '
  He snapped the steel on his prisoner's wrist,
And Ryan, hearing the handcuffs click,
  Recovered his wits as they turned to go,
For fright will sober a man as quick
  As all the drugs that the doctors know.

There was a girl in that rough bar
  Went by the name of Kate Carew
Quiet and shy as the bush girls are,
  But ready-witted and plucky, too.

She loved this Ryan, or so they say,
  And passing by, while her eyes were dim
With tears, she said in a careless way,
  'The Swagman's round in the stable, Jim.

Spoken too low for the trooper's ear,
  Why should she care if he heard or not '
Plenty of swagmen far and near,
  And yet to Ryan it meant a lot.
That was the name of the grandest horse
  In all the district from east to west
In every show ring, on every course
  They always counted the Swagman best.

He was a wonder, a raking bay—
  One of the grand old Snowdon strain—
One of the sort that could race and stay
  With his mighty limbs and his length of rein.
Born and bred on the mountain side,
  He could race through scrub like a kangaroo,
The girl herself on his back might ride,
  And the Swagman would carry her safely through.

He would travel gaily from daylight's flush
   Till after the stars hung out their lamps,
There was never his like in the open bush,
   And never his match on the cattle-camps.
For faster horses might well be found
   On racing tracks, or a plain's extent,
But few, if any, on broken ground
   Could see the way that the Swagman went.

When this girl's father, old Jim Carew,
   Was droving out on the Castlereagh
With Conroy's cattle, a wire came through
   To say that his wife couldn't live the day.
And he was a hundred miles from home,
   As flies the crow, with never a track,
Through plains as pathless as ocean's foam,
   He mounted straight on the Swagman's back.

He left the camp by the sundown light,
   And the settlers out on the Marthaguy
Awoke and heard, in the dead of night,
   A single horseman hurrying by.

He crossed the Bogan at Dandaloo,
  And many a mile of the silent plain
That lonely rider behind him threw
  Before they settled to sleep again.

He rode all night and he steered his course
  By the shining stars with a bushman's skill,
And every time that he pressed his horse
  The Swagman answered him gamely still.
He neared his home as the east was bright,
  The doctor met him outside the town :
'Carew ! How far did you come last night?'
  'A hundred miles since the sun went down.'

And his wife got round, and an oath he passed,
  So long as he or one of his breed
Could raise a coin, though it took their last
  The Swagman never should want a feed.
And Kate Carew, when her father died,
  She kept the horse and she kept him well :
The pride of the district far and wide,
  He lived in style at the bush hotel.

Such was the Swagman ; and Ryan knew
    Nothing about could pace the crack ;
Little he'd care for the man in blue
    If once he got on the Swagman's back.
But how to do it?   A word let fall
    Gave him the hint as the girl passed by ;
Nothing but ' Swagman—stable-wall ;
    ' Go to the stable and mind your eye.'

He caught her meaning, and quickly turned
    To the trooper : ' Reckon you'll gain a stripe
' By arresting me, and it's easily earned ;
    ' Let's go to the stable and get my pipe,
' The Swagman has it.'   So off they went,
    And soon as ever they turned their backs
The girl slipped down, on some errand bent
    Behind the stable, and seized an axe.

The trooper stood at the stable door
    While Ryan went in quite cool and slow,
And then (the trick had been played before)
    The girl outside gave the wall a blow.

Three slabs fell out of the stable wall—
  'Twas done 'fore ever the trooper knew—
And Ryan, as soon as he saw them fall,
  Mounted the Swagman and rushed him through.

The trooper heard the hoof-beats ring
  In the stable yard, and he slammed the gate,
But the Swagman rose with a mighty spring
  At the fence, and the trooper fired too late,
As they raced away and his shots flew wide
  And Ryan no longer need care a rap,
For never a horse that was lapped in hide
  Could catch the Swagman in Conroy's Gap.

And that's the story.   You want to know
  If Ryan came back to his Kate Carew ;
Of course he should have, as stories go.
  But the worst of it is, this story's true :
And in real life it's a certain rule,
  Whatever poets and authors say
Of high-toned robbers and all their school,
  These horsethief fellows aren't built that way.

Come back !   Don't hope it—the slinking hound,
  He sloped across to the Queensland side,
And sold the Swagman for fifty pound,
  And stole the money, and more beside.
And took to drink, and by some good chance
  Was killed—thrown out of a stolen trap.
And that was the end of this small romance,
  The end of the story of Conroy's Gap.

OUR NEW HORSE

The boys had come back from the races
    All silent and down on their luck ;
They'd backed 'em, straight out and for places,
    But never a winner they struck.
They lost their good money on Slogan,
    And fell, most uncommonly flat,
When Partner, the pride of the Bogan,
    Was beaten by Aristocrat.

And one said, ' I move that instanter
    ' We sell out our horses and quit,
' The brutes ought to win in a canter,
    ' Such trials they do when they're fit.
' The last one they ran was a snorter—
    ' A gallop to gladden one's heart—
' Two-twelve for a mile and a quarter,
    ' And finished as straight as a dart.

21

' And then when I think that they're ready
　' To win me a nice little swag,
' They are licked like the veriest neddy—
　' They're licked from the fall of the flag.
' The mare held her own to the stable,
　' She died out to nothing at that,
' And Partner he never seemed able
　' To pace it with Aristocrat.

And times have been bad, and the seasons
　' Don't promise to be of the best ;
' In short, boys, there's plenty of reasons
　' For giving the racing a rest.
' The mare can be kept on the station—
　Her breeding is good as can be—
' But Partner, his next destination
　' Is rather a trouble to me.

' We can't sell him here, for they know him
　' As well as the clerk of the course ;
' He's raced and won races till, blow him,
　' He's done as a handicap horse.

' A jady, uncertain performer,
   ' They weight him right out of the hunt,
' And clap it on warmer and warmer
   ' Whenever he gets near the front.
' It's no use to paint him or dot him
   ' Or put any ' fake ' on his brand,
' For bushmen are smart, and they'd spot him
   ' In any sale-yard in the land.
' The folk about here could all tell him,
   ' Could swear to each separate hair ;
' Let us send him to Sydney and sell him,
   ' There's plenty of Jugginses there.
' We'll call him a maiden, and treat 'em
   ' To trials will open their eyes,
' We'll run their best horses and beat 'em,
   ' And then won't they think him a prize.
' I pity the fellow that buys him,
   ' He'll find in a very short space,
' No matter how highly he tries him,
   ' The beggar won't *race* in a race.'
   .   .   .   .   .

Next week, under ' Seller and Buyer,'
   Appeared in the *Daily Gazette :*
' A racehorse for sale, and a flyer ;
   ' Has never been started as yet ;

c

' A trial will show what his pace is ;
  ' The buyer can get him in light,
' And win all the handicap races.
  ' Apply here before Wednesday night.

He sold for a hundred and thirty,
  Because of a gallop he had
One morning with Bluefish and Bertie,
  And donkey-licked both of 'em bad.
And when the old horse had departed,
  The life on the station grew tame ;
The race-track was dull and deserted,
  The boys had gone back on the game.

.   .   .   .   .   .

The winter rolled by, and the station
  Was green with the garland of spring
A spirit of glad exultation
  Awoke in each animate thing.
And all the old love, the old longing,
  Broke out in the breasts of the boys,
The visions of racing came thronging
  With all its delirious joys.

The rushing of floods in their courses,
　　The rattle of rain on the roofs
Recalled the fierce rush of the horses,
　　The thunder of galloping hoofs.
And soon one broke out : ' I can suffer
　　' No longer the life of a slug,
'The man that don't race is a duffer,
　　' Let's have one more run for the mug.'

Why, *everything* races, no matter
　　Whatever its method may be :
The waterfowl hold a regatta ;
　　The 'possums run heats up a tree ;
The emus are constantly sprinting
　　A handicap out on the plain ;
It seems like all nature was hinting,
　　'Tis time to be at it again.

The cockatoo parrots are talking
　　Of races to far away lands ;
The native companions are walking
　　A go-as-you-please on the sands ;
The little foals gallop for pastime ;
　　The wallabies race down the gap ;

Let's try it once more for the last time,
  Bring out the old jacket and cap.

And now for a horse; we might try one
  Of those that are bred on the place,
But I think it better to buy one,
  A horse that has proved he can race.
Let us send down to Sydney to Skinner,
  A thorough good judge who can ride,
And ask him to buy us a spinner
  To clean out the whole countryside.

They wrote him a letter as follows :
  'We want you to buy us a horse;
'He must have the speed to catch swallows,
  'And stamina with it of course.
'The price ain't a thing that'll grieve us,
  'It's getting a bad 'un annoys
The undersigned blokes, and believe us,
  'We're yours to a cinder, ' the boys.''

He answered : ' I've bought you a hummer,
  'A horse that has never been raced ;
'I saw him run over the Drummer,
  'He held him outclassed and outpaced.

' His breeding's not known, but they state he
  ' Is born of a thoroughbred strain,
'I paid them a hundred and eighty,
  ' And started the horse in the train.'

They met him—alas, that these verses
  Aren't up to the subject's demands—
Can't set forth their eloquent curses,
  For Partner was back on their hands.
They went in to meet him in gladness,
  They opened his box with delight—
A silent procession of sadness
  They crept to the station at night.

And life has grown dull on the station,
  The boys are all silent and slow ;
Their work is a daily vexation,
  And sport is unknown to them now.
Whenever they think how they stranded,
  They squeal just like guinea-pigs squeal ;
They bit their own hook, and were landed
  With fifty pounds loss on the deal.

AN IDYLL OF DANDALOO

On Western plains, where shade is not,
  'Neath summer skies of cloudless blue,
Where all is dry and all is hot,
  There stands the town of Dandaloo—
A township where life's total sum
Is sleep, diversified with rum.

It's grass-grown streets with dust are deep,
  'Twere vain endeavour to express
The dreamless silence of its sleep,
  Its wide, expansive drunkenness.
The yearly races mostly drew
A lively crowd to Dandaloo.

There came a sportsman from the East,
  The eastern land where sportsmen blow,
And brought with him a speedy beast—
  A speedy beast as horses go.

33

He came afar in hope to ' do '
The little town of Dandaloo.

Now this was weak of him, I wot—
   Exceeding weak, it seemed to me—
For we in Dandaloo were not
   The Jugginses we seemed to be ;
In fact, we rather thought we knew
Our book by heart in Dandaloo.

We held a meeting at the bar,
   And met the question fair and square—
' We've stumped the country near and tar
   ' To raise the cash for races here ;
' We've got a hundred pounds or two—
' Not half so bad for Dandaloo.

' And now, it seems, we have to be
   ' Cleaned out by this here Sydney bloke,
' With his imported horse ; and he
   ' Will scoop the pool and leave us broke
' Shall we sit still, and make no fuss
' While this chap climbs all over us ?

.   .   .   .   .   .

The races came to Dandaloo,
   And all the cornstalks from the West,
On ev'ry kind of moke and screw,
   Came forth in all their glory drest.
The stranger's horse, as hard as nails,
Look'd fit to run for New South Wales.

He won the race by half a length—
   Quite half a length, it seemed to me—
But Dandaloo, with all its strength,
   Roared out ' Dead heat ! ' most fervently ;
And, after hesitation meet,
The judge's verdict was ' Dead heat ! '

And many men there were could tell
   What gave the verdict extra force :
The stewards, and the judge as well—
   They all had backed the second horse.
For things like this they sometimes do
In larger towns than Dandaloo

They ran it off ; the stranger won,
   Hands down, by near a hundred yards
He smiled to think his troubles done ;
   But Dandaloo held all the cards.

They went to scale and—cruel fate !—
His jockey turned out under-weight.

Perhaps they'd tampered with the scale !
    I cannot tell.   I only know
It weighed him *out* all right.   I fail
    To paint that Sydney sportsman's woe.
He said the stewards were a crew
Of low-lived thieves in Dandaloo.

He lifted up his voice, irate,
    And swore till all the air was blue ;
So then we rose to vindicate
    The dignity of Dandaloo.
' Look here,' said we, ' you must not poke
Such oaths at us poor country folk.'

We rode him softly on a rail,
    We shied at him, in careless glee,
Some large tomatoes, rank and stale,
    And eggs of great antiquity—
Their wild, unholy fragrance flew
About the town of Dandaloo.

He left the town at break of day,
    He led his race-horse through the streets,
And now he tells the tale, they say,
    To every racing man he meets.
And Sydney sportsmen all eschew
The atmosphere of Dandaloo.

THE GEEBUNG POLO CLUB

It was somewhere up the country, in a land of rock
    and scrub,
That they formed an institution called the Geebung
    Polo Club.
They were long and wiry natives from the rugged
    mountain side.
And the horse was never saddled that the Geebungs
    couldn't ride ;
But their style of playing polo was irregular and rash—
They had mighty little science, but a mighty lot of
    dash :
And they played on mountain ponies that were
    muscular and strong,
Though their coats were quite unpolished, and their
    manes and tails were long.
And they used to train those ponies wheeling cattle
    in the scrub :
They were demons, were the members of the Geebung
    Polo Club

It was somewhere down the country, in a city's smoke
   and steam,
That a polo club existed, called 'The Cuff and Collar
   Team.'
As a social institution 'twas a marvellous success,
For the members were distinguished by exclusiveness
   and dress.
They had natty little ponies that were nice, and
   smooth, and sleek,
For their cultivated owners only rode 'em once a week.
So they started up the country in pursuit of sport
   and fame,
For they meant to show the Geebungs how they
   ought to play the game;
And they took their valets with them—just to give
   their boots a rub
Ere they started operations on the Geebung Polo
   Club.

Now my readers can imagine how the contest ebbed
   and flowed,
When the Geebung boys got going it was time to
   clear the road;
And the game was so terrific that ere· half the time
   was gone

A spectator's leg was broken—just from merely look-
 ing on.

For they waddied one another till the plain was
 strewn with dead,

While the score was kept so even that they neither
 got ahead.

And the Cuff and Collar Captain, when he tumbled
 off to die,

Was the last surviving player—so the game was
 called a tie.

Then the Captain of the Geebungs raised him slowly
 from the ground,

Though his wounds were mostly mortal, yet he fiercely
 gazed around ;

There was no one to oppose him—all the rest were in
 a trance,

So he scrambled on his pony for his last expiring
 chance,

For he meant to make an effort to get victory to his
 side ;

So he struck at goal—and missed it— then he tumbled
 off and died.

.   .   .   .   .

By the old Campaspe River, where the breezes shake
  the grass,
There's a row of little gravestones that the stockmen
  never pass,
For they bear a crude inscription saying, 'Stranger,
  drop a tear,
' For the Cuff and Collar players and the Geebung
  boys lie here.'
And on misty moonlit evenings, while the dingoes
  howl around,
You can see their shadows flitting down that phantom
  polo ground ;
You can hear the loud collisions as the flying players
  meet,
And the rattle of the mallets, and the rush of ponies'
  feet,
Till the terrified spectator rides like blazes to the
  pub—
He's been haunted by the spectres of the Geebung
  Polo Club.

THE TRAVELLING POST OFFICE

THE roving breezes come and go, the reed beds sweep
    and sway,
The sleepy river murmurs low, and loiters on its way,
It is the land of lots o' time along the Castlereagh.

.   .   .   .   .   .

The old man's son had left the farm, he found it
    dull and slow,
He drifted to the great North-west where all the
    rovers go.
' He's gone so long,' the old man said, ' he's dropped
    right out of mind,
' But if you'd write a line to him I'd take it very kind ;
' He's shearing here and fencing there, a kind of waif
    and stray,
 'He's droving now with Conroy's sheep along the
    Castlereagh.

47

'The sheep are travelling for the grass, and travelling
    very slow ;
'They may be at Mundooran now, or past the Over-
    flow,
'Or tramping down the black soil flats across by
    Waddiwong,
'But all those little country towns would send the
    letter wrong,
'The mailman, if he's extra tired, would pass them in
    his sleep,
'It's safest to address the note to 'Care of Conroy's
    sheep,'
'For five and twenty thousand head can scarcely go
    astray,
'You write to 'Care of Conroy's sheep along the
    Castlereagh.''
        .   .   .   .

By rock and ridge and riverside the western mail has
    gone,
Across the great Blue Mountain Range to take that
    letter on.
A moment on the topmost grade while open fire doors
    glare,
She pauses like a living thing to breathe the moun-
    tain air,

Then launches down the other side across the plains
away

To bear that note to ' Conroy's sheep along the Castle-
reagh.'

And now by coach and mailman's bag it goes from
town to town,

And Conroy's Gap and Conroy's Creek have marked
it ' further down.'

Beneath a sky of deepest blue where never cloud
abides,

A speck upon the waste of plain the lonely mailman
rides.

Where fierce hot winds have set the pine and myall
boughs asweep

He hails the shearers passing by for news of Conroy's
sheep.

By big lagoons where wildfowl play and crested
pigeons flock,

By camp fires where the drovers ride around their
restless stock,

And past the teamster toiling down to fetch the wool
away

My letter chases Conroy's sheep along the Castlereagh.

SALTBUSH BILL

Now this is the law of the Overland that all in the
    West obey,
A man must cover with travelling sheep a six-mile
    stage a day ;
But this is the law which the drovers make, right
    easily understood,
They travel their stage where the grass is bad, but
    they camp where the grass is good ;
They camp, and they ravage the squatter's grass till
    never a blade remains,
Then they drift away as the white clouds drift on the
    edge of the saltbush plains,
From camp to camp and from run to run they battle
    it hand to hand,
For a blade of grass and the right to pass on the
    track of the Overland.

For this is the law of the Great Stock Routes, 'tis
    written in white and black—
The man that goes with a travelling mob must keep
    to a half-mile track ;
And the drovers keep to a half-mile track on the runs
    where the grass is dead,
But they spread their sheep on a well-grassed run till
    they go with a two-mile spread.
So the squatters hurry the drovers on from dawn till
    the fall of night,
And the squatters' dogs and the drovers' dogs get
    mixed in a deadly fight ;
Yet the squatters' men, though they hunt the mob,
    are willing the peace to keep,
For the drovers learn how to use their hands when
    they go with the travelling sheep ;
But this is the tale of a Jackaroo that came from a
    foreign strand,
And the fight that he fought with Saltbush Bill, the
    King of the Overland.

Now Saltbush Bill was a drover tough, as ever the
    country knew,
He had fought his way on the Great Stock Routes
    from the sea to the big Barcoo;

He could tell when he came to a friendly run that
    gave him a chance to spread,
And he knew where the hungry owners were that
    hurried his sheep ahead ;
He was drifting down in the Eighty drought with a
    mob that could scarcely creep,
(When the kangaroos by the thousands starve, it is
    rough on the travelling sheep),
And he camped one night at the crossing-place on the
    edge of the Wilga run,
' We must manage a feed for them here,' he said, ' or
    the half of the mob are done ! ' '
So he spread them out when they left the camp
    wherever they liked to go,
Till he grew aware of a Jackaroo with a station-hand
    in tow,
And they set to work on the straggling sheep, and
    with many a stockwhip crack
They forced them in where the grass was dead in the
    space of the half-mile track ;
So William prayed that the hand of fate might
    suddenly strike him blue
But he'd get some grass for his starving sheep in the
    teeth of that Jackaroo.

So he turned and he cursed the Jackaroo, he cursed
    him alive or dead,
From the soles of his great unwieldy feet to the
    crown of his ugly head,
With an extra curse on the moke he rode and the cur
    at his heels that ran,
Till the Jackaroo from his horse got down and he
    went for the drover-man ;
With the station-hand for his picker-up, though the
    sheep ran loose the while,
They battled it out on the saltbush plain in tne
    regular prize-ring style.

Now, the new chum fought for his honour's sake and
    the pride of the English race,
But the drover fought for his daily bread with a
    smile on his bearded face ;
So he shifted ground and he sparred for wind and he
    made it a lengthy mill,
And from time to time as his scouts came in they
    whispered to Saltbush Bill—
We have spread the sheep with a two-mile spread,
    and the grass it is something grand,
You must stick to him, Bill, for another round for
    the pride of the Overland.'

The new chum made it a rushing fight, though never
    a blow got home,
Till the sun rode high in the cloudless sky and glared
    on the brick-red loam,
Till the sheep drew in to the shelter-trees and settled
    them down to rest,
Then the drover said he would fight no more and he
    gave his opponent best.
So the new chum rode to the homestead straight and
    he told them a story grand
Of the desperate fight that he fought that day with
    the King of the Overland.
And the tale went home to the Public Schools of the
    pluck of the English swell,
How the drover fought for his very life, but blood in
    the end must tell.
But the travelling sheep and the Wilga sheep were
    boxed on the Old Man Plain.
'Twas a full week's work ere they drafted out and
    hunted them off again,
With a week's good grass in their wretched hides.
    with a curse and a stockwhip crack,
They hunted them off on the road once more to starve
    on the half-mile track.

And Saltbush Bill, on the Overland, will many a
    time recite

How the best day's work that ever he did was the
    day that he lost the fight.

A MOUNTAIN STATION

I BOUGHT a run a while ago,
  On country rough and ridgy,
Where wallaroos and wombats grow—
  The Upper Murrumbidgee.
The grass is rather scant, it's true,
  But this a fair exchange is,
The sheep can see a lovely view
  By climbing up the ranges.

And 'She-oak Flat' 's the station's name,
  I'm not surprised at that, sirs:
The oaks were there before I came,
  And I supplied the flat, sirs.
A man would wonder how it's done,
  The stock so soon decreases—
They sometimes tumble off the run
  And break themselves to pieces.

56

A MOUNTAIN STATION 57

I've tried to make expenses meet.
    But wasted all my labours,
The sheep the dingoes didn't eat
    Were stolen by the neighbours.
They stole my pears —my native pears—
    Those thrice-convicted felons,
And ravished from me unawares
    My crop of paddy-melons.

And sometimes under sunny skies,
    Without an explanation,
The Murrumbidgee used to rise
    And overflow the station.
But this was caused (as now I know)
    When summer sunshine glowing
Had melted all Kiandra's snow
    And set the river going.

And in the news, perhaps you read:
    'Stock passings.   Puckawidgee,
'Fat cattle : Seven hundred head
    'Swept down the Murrumbidgee ;
'Their destination's quite obscure,
    ' But, somehow, there's a notion,
' Unless the river falls, they're sure
    'To reach the Southern Ocean.'

So after that I'll give it best;
  No more with Fate I'll battle.
I'll let the river take the rest,
  For those were all my cattle.
And with one comprehensive curse
  I close my brief narration,
And advertise it in my verse—
  'For Sale ! A Mountain Station.'

BEEN THERE BEFORE

THERE came a stranger to Walgett town,
  To Walgett town when the sun was low,
And he carried a thirst that was worth a crown,
  Yet how to quench it he did not know ;
But he thought he might take those yokels down,
The guileless yokels of Walgett town.

They made him a bet in a private bar,
  In a private bar when the talk was high,
And they bet him some pounds no matter how far
  He could pelt a stone, yet he could not shy
A stone right over the river so brown,
The Darling river at Walgett town.

He knew that the river from bank to bank
  Was fifty yards, and he smiled a smile
As he trundled down, but his hopes they sank
  For there wasn't a stone within fifty mile ;
For the saltbush plain and the open down
Produce no quarries in Walgett town.

59

The yokels laughed at his hopes o'erthrown,
    And he stood awhile like a man in a dream ;
Then out of his pocket he fetched a stone,
    And pelted it over the silent stream—
He had been there before : he had wandered down
On a previous visit to Walgett town.

THE MAN WHO WAS AWAY

THE widow sought the lawyer's room with children
  three in tow,
She told the lawyer man her tale in tones of deepest
  woe.
Said she, 'My husband took to drink for pains in his
  inside,
'And never drew a sober breath from then until he
  died.

'He never drew a sober breath, he died without a
  will,
'And I must sell the bit of land the childer's mouths
  to fill.
'There's some is grown and gone away, but some is
  childer yet,
'And times is very bad indeed—a livin's hard to get.

61

'There's Min and Sis and little Chris, they stops at
    home with me,
'And Sal has married Greenhide Bill that breaks for
    Bingeree.
And Fred is drovin' Conroy's sheep along the Castle-
    reagh,
And Charley's shearin' down the Bland, and Peter
    is away.'

The lawyer wrote the details down in ink of legal
    blue—
'There's Minnie, Susan, Christopher, they stop at
    home with you;
'There's Sarah, Frederick, and Charles, I'll write to
    them to-day,
'But what about the other one--the one who is away?

'You'll have to furnish his consent to sell the bit of
    land.'
The widow shuffled in her seat, 'Oh, don't you under-
    stand?
'I thought a lawyer ought to know—I don't know
    what to say—
'You'll have to do without him, boss, for Peter is
    away.'

But here the little boy spoke up—said he, ' We
    thought you knew ;
' He's done six months in Goulburn gaol—he's got
    six more to do.'
Thus in one comprehensive flash he made it clear as
    day,
The mystery of Peter's life—the man who was away.

THE MAN FROM IRONBARK

It was the man from Ironbark who struck the Sydney
    town,
He wandered over street and park, he wandered up
    and down.
He loitered here, he loitered there, till he was like to
    drop,
Until at last in sheer despair he sought a barber's
    shop.
'Ere! shave my beard and whiskers off, I'll be a
    man of mark,
' I'll go and do the Sydney toff up home in Ironbark.'

The barber man was small and flash, as barbers
    mostly are,
He wore a strike-your-fancy sash, he smoked a huge
    cigar :
He was a humorist of note and keen at repartee,
He laid the odds and kept a 'tote,' whatever that
    may be,

64

And when he saw our friend arrive, he whispered
  'Here's a lark !
'Just watch me catch him all alive, this man from
  Ironbark.'

There were some gilded youths that sat along the
  barber's wall.
Their eyes were dull, their heads were flat, they had
  no brains at all ;
To them the barber passed the wink, his dexter eyelid
  shut,
'I'll make this bloomin' yokel think his bloomin'
  throat is cut.'
And as he soaped and rubbed it in he made a rude
  remark :
' I s'pose the flats is pretty green up there in Iron-
  bark.'

A grunt was all reply he got ; he shaved the bush-
  man's chin,
Then made the water boiling hot and dipped the razor
  in.
He raised his hand, his brow grew black, he paused
  awhile to gloat,

B

Then slashed the red-hot razor-back across his victim's
throat ;
Upon the newly-shaven skin it made a livid mark—
No doubt it fairly took him in—the man from Iron-
bark.

He fetched a wild up-country yell might wake the
dead to hear,
And though his throat, he knew full well, was cut
from ear to ear,
He struggled gamely to his feet, and faced the
murd'rous foe :
'You've done for me! you dog, I'm beat! one hit
before I go !
'I only wish I had a knife, you blessed murdering
shark !
'But you'll remember all your life, the man from
Ironbark.'

He lifted up his hairy paw, with one tremendous clout
He landed on the barber's jaw, and knocked the
barber out.
He set to work with tooth and nail, he made the
place a wreck ;
He grabbed the nearest gilded youth, and tried to
break his neck.

And all the while his throat he held to save his vital
    spark,
And 'Murder! Bloody Murder!' yelled the man from
    Ironbark.

A peeler man who heard the din came in to see the
    show;
He tried to run the bushman in, but he refused to go.
And when at last the barber spoke, and said ''Twas
    all in fun—
' 'Twas just a little harmless joke, a trifle overdone.'
' A joke!' he cried, ' By George, that's fine ; a lively
    sort of lark ;
' I'd like to catch that murdering swine some night
    in Ironbark.'

And now while round the shearing floor the list'ning
    shearers gape,
He tells the story o'er and o'er, and brags of his
    escape.
' Them barber chaps what keeps a tote, By George,
    I've had enough,
' One tried to cut my bloomin' throat, but thank the
    Lord it's tough.'

And whether he's believed or no, there's one thing to
   remark,
That flowing beards are all the go way up in Ironbark.

THE OPEN STEEPLECHASE

I HAD ridden over hurdles up the country once or
  twice,
By the side of Snowy River with a horse they called
  ' The Ace.'
And we brought him down to Sydney, and our rider
  Jimmy Rice,
Got a fall and broke his shoulder, so they nabbed me
  in a trice—
Me, that never wore the colours, for the Open Steeple-
  chase.

'Make the running,' said the trainer, 'it's your only
  chance whatever,
'Make it hot from start to finish, for the old black
  horse can stay,
'And just think of how they'll take it, when they
  hear on Snowy River

69

'That the country boy was plucky, and the country
    horse was clever.

'You must ride for old Monaro and the mountain
    boys to-day.'

'Are you ready?' said the starter, as we held the
    horses back,
All ablazing with impatience, with excitement all
    aglow ;
Before us like a ribbon stretched the steeplechasing
    track,
And the sun-rays glistened brightly on the chestnut
    and the black
As the starter's words came slowly, 'Are—you—
    ready? Go!'

Well, I scarcely knew we'd started, I was stupid like
    with wonder
Till the field closed up beside me and a jump appeared
    ahead.
And we flew it like a hurdle, not a baulk and not a
    blunder,
As we charged it all together, and it fairly whistled
    under,
And then some were pulled behind me and a few
    shot out and led.

So we ran for half the distance, and I'm making no
    pretences
When I tell you I was feeling very nervous-like and
    queer,
For those jockeys rode like demons ; you would think
    they'd lost their senses
If you saw them rush their horses at those rasping
    five foot fences—
And in place of making running I was falling to the
    rear.

Till a chap came racing past me on a horse they
    called 'The Quiver,'
And said he, 'My country joker, are you going to
    give it best ?
'Are you frightened of the fences ? does their stout-
    ness make you shiver ?
'Have they come to breeding cowards by the side of
    Snowy River ?
'Are there riders on Monaro ?——' but I never heard
    the rest.

For I drove the Ace and sent him just as fast as he
    could pace it,
At the big black line of timber stretching fair across
    the track,

And he shot beside the Quiver. 'Now,' said I, 'my
    boy, we'll race it.
'You can come with Snowy River if you're only game
    to face it ,
'Let us mend the pace a little and we'll see who cries
    a crack.'

So we raced away together, and we left the others
    standing,
And the people cheered and shouted as we settled
    down to ride,
And we clung beside the Quiver. At his taking off
    and landing
I could see his scarlet nostril and his mighty ribs
    expanding,
And the Ace stretched out in earnest and we held
    him stride for stride.

But the pace was so terrific that they soon ran out
    their tether—
They were rolling in their gallop, they were fairly
    blown and beat—
But they both were game as pebbles—neither one
    would show the feather.

And we rushed them at the fences, and they cleared
    them both together,
Nearly every time they clouted, but they somehow
    kept their feet.

Then the last jump rose before us, and they faced it
    game as ever—
We were both at spur and whipcord, fetching blood
    at every bound—
And above the people's cheering and the cries of
    ' Ace ' and ' Quiver,'
I could hear the trainer shouting, ' One more run for
    Snowy River.'
Then we struck the jump together and came smashing
    to the ground.

Well, the Quiver ran to blazes, but the Ace stood still
    and waited,
Stood and waited like a statue while I scrambled on
    his back.
There was no one next or near me for the field was
    fairly slated,
So I cantered home a winner with my shoulder
    dislocated,
While the man that rode the Quiver followed limping
    down the track.

And he shook my hand and told me that in all his
    days he never

Met a man who rode more gamely, and our last set
    to was prime,

And we wired them on Monaro how we chanced to
    beat the Quiver.

And they sent us back an answer, 'Good old sort
    from Snowy River :

'Send us word each race you start in and we'll
    back you every time.'

THE AMATEUR RIDER

Him going to ride for us! *Him*—with the pants and
    the eyeglass and all.
Amateur! don't he just look it—it's twenty to one on
    a fall.
Boss must be gone off his head to be sending our
    steeplechase crack
Out over fences like these with an object like that on
    his back.

Ride! Don't tell *me* he can ride. With his pants
    just as loose as balloons,
How can he sit on his horse? and his spurs like a pair
    of harpoons;
Ought to be under the Dog Act, he ought, and be
    kept off the course.
Fall! why, he'd fall off a cart, let alone off a steeple-
    chase horse.

      .   .   .   .   .   .

75

Yessir! the 'orse is all ready—I wish you'd have rode
    him before;
Nothing like knowing your 'orse, sir, and this chap's
    a terror to bore;
Battleaxe always could pull, and he rushes his fences
    like fun—
Stands off his jump twenty feet, and then springs like
    a shot from a gun.

Oh, he can jump 'em all right, sir, you make no mis-
    take, 'e's a toff;
Clouts 'em in earnest, too, sometimes, you mind that
    he don't clout you off—
Don't seem to mind how he hits 'em, his shins is as
    hard as a nail,
Sometimes you'll see the fence shake and the splinters
    fly up from the rail.

All you can do is to hold him and just let him jump
    as he likes,
Give him his head at the fences, and hang on like
    death if he strikes;
Don't let him run himself out—you can lie third or
    fourth in the race—
Until you clear the stone wall, and from that you can
    put on the pace.

Fell at that wall once, he did, and it gave him a
    regular spread,
Ever since that time he flies it—he'll stop if you pull
    at his head,
Just let him race—you can trust him—he'll take first-
    class care he don't fall,
And I think that's the lot—but remember, *he must
    have his head at the wall.*

·   ·   ·   ·   ·   ·

Well, he's down safe as far as the start, and he seems
    to sit on pretty neat,
Only his baggified breeches would ruinate anyone's
    seat—
They're away—here they come—the first fence, and
    he's head over heels for a crown !
Good for the new chum, he's over, and two of the
    others are down !

Now for the treble, my hearty—By Jove, he can ride,
    after all ;
Whoop, that's your sort—let him fly them ! He hasn't
    much fear of a fall.

Who in the world would have thought it? And
    aren't they just going a pace?
Little Recruit in the lead there will make it a stoutly-
    run race.

Lord! But they're racing in earnest—and down goes
    Recruit on his head,
Rolling clean over his boy—it's a miracle if he ain't
    dead.
Battleaxe, Battleaxe, yet! By the Lord, he's got most
    of 'em beat—
Ho! did you see how he struck, and the swell never
    moved in his seat?

Second time round, and, by Jingo! he's holding his
    lead of 'em well;
Hark to him clouting the timber! It don't seem to
    trouble the swell.
Now for the wall—let him rush it. A thirty-foot
    leap, I declare—
Never a shift in his seat, and he's racing for home
    like a hare.

What's that that's chasing him—Rataplan—regular
    demon to stay!

Sit down and ride for your life now! Oh, good, that's
    the style—come away!
Rataplan's certain to beat you, unless you can give
    him the slip;
Sit down and rub in the whalebone now—give him
    the spurs and the whip!

Battleaxe, Battleaxe, yet—and it's Battleaxe wins for
    a crown;
Look at him rushing the fences, he wants to bring
    t'other chap down.
Rataplan never will catch him if only he keeps on his
    pins;
Now! the last fence! and he's over it! Battleaxe
    Battleaxe wins!

    .   .   .   .   .   .

Well, sir, you rode him just perfect—I knew from the
    first you could ride.
Some of the chaps said you couldn't, an' I says just
    like this a' one side:
Mark me, I says, that's a tradesman—the saddle is
    where he was bred.
Weight! you're all right, sir, and thank you; **and**
    them was the words that I said.

ON KILEY'S RUN

THE roving breezes come and go
              On Kiley's Run,
The sleepy river murmurs low,
And far away one dimly sees
Beyond the stretch of forest trees—
Beyond the foothills dusk and dun—
The ranges sleeping in the sun
              On Kiley's Run.

'Tis many years since first I came
              To Kiley's Run,
More years than I would care to name
Since I, a stripling, used to ride
For miles and miles at Kiley's side,
The while in stirring tones he told
The stories of the days of old
              On Kiley's Run.

I see the old bush homestead now
        On Kiley's Run,
Just nestled down beneath the brow
Of one small ridge above the sweep
Of river-flat, where willows weep
And jasmine flowers and roses bloom,
The air was laden with perfume
        On Kiley's Run.

We lived the good old station life
        On Kiley's Run,
With little thought of care or strife.
Old Kiley seldom used to roam,
He liked to make the Run his home,
The swagman never turned away
With empty hand at close of day
        From Kiley's Run.

We kept a racehorse now and then
        On Kiley's Run,
And neighb'ring stations brought their men
To meetings where the sport was free,
And dainty ladies came to see
Their champions ride ; with laugh and song
The old house rang the whole night long
        On Kiley's Run.

The station hands were friends I wot
      On Kiley's Run,
A reckless, merry-hearted lot—
All splendid riders, and they knew
The ' boss ' was kindness through and through.
Old Kiley always stood their friend,
And so they served him to the end
      On Kiley's Run.

But droughts and losses came apace
      To Kiley's Run,
Till ruin stared him in the face ;
He toiled and toiled while lived the light,
He dreamed of overdrafts at night :
At length, because he could not pay,
His bankers took the stock away
      From Kiley's Run.

Old Kiley stood and saw them go
      From Kiley's Run.
The well-bred cattle marching slow ;
His stockmen, mates for many a day,
They wrung his hand and went away.

Too old to make another start,
Old Kiley died—of broken heart,
On Kiley's Run.

. . . . . .

The owner lives in England now
Of Kiley's Run.
He knows a racehorse from a cow;
But that is all he knows of stock:
His chiefest care is how to dock
Expenses, and he sends from town
To cut the shearers' wages down
On Kiley's Run.

There are no neighbours anywhere
Near Kiley's Run.
The hospitable homes are bare,
The gardens gone; for no pretence
Must hinder cutting down expense:
The homestead that we held so dear
Contains a half-paid overseer
On Kiley's Run.

All life and sport and hope have died
On Kiley's Run.
No longer there the stockmen ride;

For sour-faced boundary riders creep
On mongrel horses after sheep,
Through ranges where, at racing speed,
Old Kiley used to ' wheel the lead '
            On Kiley's Run.

There runs a lane for thirty miles
            Through Kiley's Run.
On either side the herbage smiles,
But wretched trav'lling sheep must pass
Without a drink or blade of grass
Thro' that long lane of death and shame :
The weary drovers curse the name
            Of Kiley's Run.

The name itself is changed of late
            Of Kiley's Run.
They call it ' Chandos Park Estate.'
The lonely swagman through the dark
Must hump his swag past Chandos Park
The name is English, don't you see,
The old name sweeter sounds to me
            Of ' Kiley's Run.'

I cannot guess what fate will bring
   To Kiley's Run—
For chances come and changes ring—
I scarcely think 'twill always be
Locked up to suit an absentee;
And if he lets it out in farms
His tenants soon will carry arms
   On Kiley's Run.

FRYING PAN'S THEOLOGY

SCENE : On Monaro.
  Dramatis Personæ :
Shock-headed blackfellow,
  Boy (on a pony).
Snowflakes are falling
  So gentle and slow,
Youngster says, ' Frying Pan,
  ' What makes it snow ? '
Frying Pan confident
  Makes the reply—
' Shake 'em big flour bag
  ' Up in the sky ! '
' What ! when there's miles of it !
  ' Sur'ly that's brag.
' Who is there strong enough
  ' Shake such a bag ? '
' What parson tellin' you,

86

'Ole Mister Dodd,
' Tell you in Sunday-school?
' Big feller God!
' He drive His bullock dray,
' Then thunder go,
' He shake His flour bag—
' Tumble down snow!'

THE TWO DEVINES

It was shearing-time at the Myall Lake,
    And there rose the sound thro' the livelong day
Of the constant clash that the shear-blades make
    When the fastest shearers are making play,
But there wasn't a man in the shearers' lines
That could shear a sheep with the two Devines.

They had rung the sheds of the east and west,
    Had beaten the cracks of the Walgett side,
And the Cooma shearers had giv'n them best—
    When they saw them shear, they were satisfied.
From the southern slopes to the western pines
They were noted men, were the two Devines.

'Twas a wether flock that had come to hand,
    Great struggling brutes, that the shearers shirk,
For the fleece was filled with the grass and sand,
    And seventy sheep was a big day's work.
' At a pound a hundred it's dashed hard lines
' To shear such sheep,' said the two Devines.

88

But the shearers knew that they'd make a cheque
　　When they came to deal with the station ewes ;
They were bare of belly and bare of neck
　　With a fleece as light as a kangaroo's.
We will show the boss how a shear-blade shines
'When we reach those ewes,' said the two Devines.

But it chanced next day when the stunted pines
　　Were swayed and stirred with the dawn-wind's
　　　　breath,
That a message came for the two Devines
　　That their father lay at the point of death.
So away at speed through the whispering pines
Down the bridle track rode the two Devines.

It was fifty miles to their father's hut,
　　And the dawn was bright when they rode away ;
At the fall of night when the shed was shut
　　And the men had rest from the toilsome day,
To the shed once more through the dark'ning pines
On their weary steeds came the two Devines.

'Well, you're back right sudden,' the super. said
　　' Is the old man dead and the funeral done ? '
　　Well, no, sir, he ain't not exactly dead,

'But as good as dead,' said the eldest son—
'And we couldn't bear such a chance to lose,
'So we came straight back to tackle the ewes.'

. . . . . .

They are shearing ewes at the Myall Lake,
   And the shed is merry the livelong day
With the clashing sound that the shear-blades make
   When the fastest shearers are making play,
And a couple of 'hundred and ninety-nines'
Are the tallies made by the two Devines.

IN THE DROVING DAYS

'ONLY a pound,' said the auctioneer,
'Only a pound ; and I'm standing here
'Selling this animal, gain or loss.
'Only a pound for the drover's horse ;
'One of the sort that was never afraid,
'One of the boys of the Old Brigade ;
'Thoroughly honest and game, I'll swear,
'Only a little the worse for wear ;
'Plenty as bad to be seen in town,
'Give me a bid and I'll knock him down ;
'Sold as he stands, and without recourse,
'Give me a bid for the drover's horse.'

Loitering there in an aimless way
Somehow I noticed the poor old grey,
Weary and battered and screwed, of course,
Yet when I noticed the old grey horse,
The rough bush saddle, and single rein
Of the bridle laid on his tangled mane,

Straightway the crowd and the auctioneer
Seemed on a sudden to disappear,
Melted away in a kind of haze,
For my heart went back to the droving days.

Back to the road, and I crossed again
Over the miles of the saltbush plain—
The shining plain that is said to be
The dried-up bed of an inland sea,
Where the air so dry and so clear and bright
Refracts the sun with a wondrous light,
And out in the dim horizon makes
The deep blue gleam of the phantom lakes.

At dawn of day we would feel the breeze
That stirred the boughs of the sleeping trees,
And brought a breath of the fragrance rare
That comes and goes in that scented air ;
For the trees and grass and the shrubs contain
A dry sweet scent on the saltbush plain.
For those that love it and understand,
The saltbush plain is a wonderland.
A wondrous country, where Nature's ways
Were revealed to me in the droving days.

We saw the fleet wild horses pass,
And the kangaroos through the Mitchell grass,
The emu ran with her frightened brood
All unmolested and unpursued.
But there rose a shout and a wild hubbub
When the dingo raced for his native scrub,
And he paid right dear for his stolen meals
With the drover's dogs at his wretched heels.
For we ran him down at a rattling pace,
While the packhorse joined in the stirring chase.
And a wild halloo at the kill we'd raise—
We were light of heart in the droving days.

'Twas a drover's horse, and my hand again
Made a move to close on a fancied rein.
For I felt the swing and the easy stride
Of the grand old horse that I used to ride
In drought or plenty, in good or ill,
That same old steed was my comrade still ;
The old grey horse with his honest ways
Was a mate to me in the droving days.

When we kept our watch in the cold and damp,
If the cattle broke from the sleeping camp,
Over the flats and across the plain,

With my head bent down on his waving mane,
Through the boughs above and the stumps below
On the darkest night I could let him go
At a racing speed; he would choose his course,
And my life was safe with the old grey horse.
But man and horse had a favourite job,
When an outlaw broke from a station mob,
With a right good will was the stockwhip plied,
As the old horse raced at the straggler's side,
And the greenhide whip such a weal would raise,
We could use the whip in the droving days.

     .   .   .   .   .   .

'Only a pound!' and was this the end—
Only a pound for the drover's friend.
The drover's friend that had seen his day,
And now was worthless, and cast away
With a broken knee and a broken heart
To be flogged and starved in a hawker's cart.
Well, I made a bid for a sense of shame
And the memories dear of the good old game.

'Thank you? Guinea! and cheap at that!
'Against you there in the curly hat!
'Only a guinea, and one more chance,

' Down he goes if there's no advance,
' Third, and the last time, one ! two ! three !'
And the old grey horse was knocked down to me.
And now he's wandering, fat and sleek,
On the lucerne flats by the Homestead Creek ;
I dare not ride him for fear he'd fall,
But he does a journey to beat them all,
For though he scarcely a trot can raise,
He can take me back to the droving days.

LOST

'HE ought to be home,' said the old man, 'without
    there's something amiss.
'He only went to the Two-mile—he ought to be back
    by this.
'He *would* ride the Reckless filly, he *would* have his
    wilful way ;
'And, here, he's not back at sundown—and what will
    his mother say ?

'He was always his mother's idol, since ever his father
    died ;
'And there isn't a horse on the station that he isn't
    game to ride.
'But that Reckless mare is vicious, and if once she
    gets away
'He hasn't got strength to hold her—and what will
    his mother say ?'

The old man walked to the sliprail, and peered up the
    dark'ning track,
And looked and longed for the rider that would never
    more come back ;
And the mother came and clutched him, with sudden,
    spasmodic fright :
' What has become of my Willie ?—why isn't he home
    to-night ? '

Away in the gloomy ranges, at the foot of an iron-
    bark,
The bonnie, winsome laddie was lying stiff and stark ;
For the Reckless mare had smashed him against a
    leaning limb,
And his comely face was battered, and his merry eyes
    were dim.

And the thoroughbred chestnut filly, the saddle be-
    neath her flanks,
Was away like fire through the ranges to join the wild
    mob's ranks ;
And a broken-hearted woman and an old man worn
    and grey
Were searching all night in the ranges till the sunrise
    brought the day.

And the mother kept feebly calling, with a hope that
    would not die,
'Willie! where are you, Willie?'   But how can the
    dead reply;
And hope died out with the daylight, and the dark-
    ness brought despair,
God pity the stricken mother, and answer the widow's
    prayer!

Though far and wide they sought him, they found
    not where he fell;
For the ranges held him precious, and guarded their
    treasure well.
The wattle blooms above him, and the blue bells blow
    close by,
And the brown bees buzz the secret, and the wild
    birds sing reply.

But the mother pined and faded, and cried, and took
    no rest,
And rode each day to the ranges on her hopeless,
    weary quest.
Seeking her loved one ever, she faded and pined away,
But with strength of her great affection she still
    sought every day.

' I know that sooner or later I shall find my boy,
    she said.
But she came not home one evening, and they found
    her lying dead,
And stamped on the poor pale features, as the spirit
    homeward pass'd,
Was an angel smile of gladness—she had found the
    boy at last.

OVER THE RANGE

LITTLE bush maiden, wondering-eyed,
  Playing alone in the creek-bed dry,
In the small green flat on every side
  Walled in by the Moonbi ranges high ;
Tell us the tale of your lonely life,
  'Mid the great grey forests that know no change
I never have left my home,' she said,
  ' I have never been over the Moonbi Range.

' Father and mother are both long dead,
  ' And I live with granny in yon wee place.'
' Where are your father and mother ?' we said.
  She puzzled awhile with thoughtful face,
Then a light came into the shy brown eye,
  And she smiled, for she thought the question
    strange
On a thing so certain—' When people die
  ' They go to the country over the range.'

'And what is this country like, my lass?'
  'There are blossoming trees and pretty flowers,
'And shining creeks where the golden grass
  'Is fresh and sweet from the summer showers.
'They never need work, nor want, nor weep;
  'No troubles can come their hearts to estrange.
'Some summer night I shall fall asleep,
  'And wake in the country over the range.'

Child, you are wise in your simple trust,
  For the wisest man knows no more than you
Ashes to ashes, and dust to dust:
  Our views by a range are bounded too;
But we know that God hath this gift in store,
  That when we come to the final change,
We shall meet with our loved ones gone before
  To the beautiful country over the range.

ONLY A JOCKEY

'Richard Bennison, a jockey, aged 14, while riding William Tell in his training, was thrown and killed. The horse is luckily uninjured.'—Melbourne Wire.

OUT in the grey cheerless chill of the morning light,
　Out on the track where the night shades still lurk;
Ere the first gleam of the sungod's returning light,
　Round come the race-horses early at work.

Reefing and pulling and racing so readily,
　Close sit the jockey-boys holding them hard,
'Steady the stallion there—canter him steadily,
　'Don't let him gallop so much as a yard.'

Fiercely he fights while the others run wide of him,
　Reefs at the bit that would hold him in thrall,
Plunges and bucks till the boy that's astride of him
　Goes to the ground with a terrible fall.

'Stop him there! Block him there! Drive him in care-
          fully,
    'Lead him about till he's quiet and cool.
'Sound as a bell! though he's blown himself fearfully,
    'Now let us pick up this poor little fool.

'Stunned? Oh, by Jove, I'm afraid it's a case with
          him ;
    'Ride for the doctor! keep bathing his head!
Send for a cart to go down to our place with him '—
    No use! One long sigh and the little chap's dead.

Only a jockey-boy, foul-mouthed and bad you see,
    Ignorant, heathenish, gone to his rest.
Parson or Presbyter, Pharisee, Sadducee,
    What did you do for him ?—bad was the best.

Negroes and foreigners, all have a claim on you;
    Yearly you send your well-advertised hoard,
But the poor jockey-boy—shame on you, shame on
          you,
    'Feed ye, my little ones '—what said the Lord ?

Him ye held less than the outer barbarian,
    Left him to die in his ignorant sin ;

Have you no principles, humanitarian?
  Have you no precept—'go gather them in?'

     .   .   .   .   .   .

Knew he God's name?   In his brutal profanity,
  That name was an oath—out of many but one—
What did he get from our famed Christianity?
  Where has his soul—if he had any—gone?

Fourteen years old, and what was he taught of it?
  What did he know of God's infinite grace?
Draw the dark curtain of shame o'er the thought of it,
  Draw the shroud over the jockey-boy's face.

HOW M'GINNIS WENT MISSING

LET us cease our idle chatter,
  Let the tears bedew our cheek,
For a man from Tallangatta
  Has been missing for a week.

Where the roaring flooded Murray
  Covered all the lower land,
There he started in a hurry,
  With a bottle in his hand.

And his fate is hid for ever,
  But the public seem to think
That he slumbered by the river,
  'Neath the influence of drink.

And they scarcely seem to wonder
  That the river, wide and deep,
Never woke him with its thunder,
  Never stirred him in his sleep.

As the crashing logs came sweeping,
  And their tumult filled the air,
Then M'Ginnis murmured, sleeping,
  ' 'Tis a wake in ould Kildare.'

So the river rose and found him
  Sleeping softly by the stream,
And the cruel waters drowned him
  Ere he wakened from his dream.

And the blossom-tufted wattle,
  Blooming brightly on the lea,
Saw M'Ginnis and the bottle
  Going drifting out to sea.

A VOICE FROM THE TOWN

A sequel to ' A Voice from the Bush'

I THOUGHT, in the days of the droving,
    Of steps I might hope to retrace,
To be done with the bush and the roving
    And settle once more in my place.
With a heart that was well nigh to breaking,
    In the long, lonely rides on the plain,
I thought of the pleasure of taking
    The hand of a lady again.

I am back into civilisation,
    Once more in the stir and the strife,
But the old joys have lost their sensation—
    The light has gone out of my life;
The men of my time they have married,
    Made fortunes or gone to the wall;
Too long from the scene I have tarried,
    And, somehow, I'm out of it all.

For I go to the balls and the races
    A lonely companionless elf,
And the ladies bestow all their graces
    On others less grey than myself ;
While the talk goes around I'm a dumb one
    'Midst youngsters that chatter and prate,
And they call me ' the Man who was Someone
    Way back in the year Sixty-eight.'

And I look, sour and old, at the dancers
    That swing to the strains of the band,
And the ladies all give me the Lancers,
    No waltzes—I quite understand.
For matrons intent upon matching
    Their daughters with infinite push,.
Would scarce think him worthy the catching,
    The broken-down man from the bush.

New partners have come and new faces,
    And I, of the bygone brigade,
Sharply feel that oblivion my place is—
    I must lie with the rest in the shade.
And the youngsters, fresh-featured and pleasant,
    They live as we lived—fairly fast ;
But I doubt if the men of the present
    Are as good as the men of the past.

Of excitement and praise they are chary,
  There is nothing much good upon earth ;
Their watchword is *nil admirari*,
  They are bored from the days of their birth.
Where the life that we led was a revel
  They ' wince and relent and refrain '—
I could show them the road—to the devil,
  Were I only a youngster again.

I could show them the road where the stumps are
  The pleasures that end in remorse,
And the game where the Devil's three trumps are,
  The woman, the card, and the horse.
Shall the blind lead the blind—shall the sower
  Of wind reap the storm as of yore ?
Though they get to their goal somewhat slower,
  They march where we hurried before.

For the world never learns—just as we did,
  They gallantly go to their fate,
Unheeded all warnings, unheeded
  The maxims of elders sedate.
As the husbandman, patiently toiling,
  Draws a harvest each year from the soil,
So the fools grow afresh for the spoiling,
  And a new crop of thieves for the spoil.

But a truce to this dull moralising,
   Let them drink while the drops are of gold,
I have tasted the dregs—'twere surprising
   Were the new wine to me like the old ;
And I weary for lack of employment
   In idleness day after day,
For the key to the door of enjoyment
   Is Youth—and I've thrown it away.

A BUNCH OF ROSES

Roses ruddy and roses white,
   What are the joys that my heart discloses?
Sitting alone in the fading light
Memories come to me here to-night
   With the wonderful scent of the big red roses.

Memories come as the daylight fades
   Down on the hearth where the firelight dozes;
Flicker and flutter the lights and shades,
And I see the face of a queen of maids
   Whose memory comes with the scent of roses.

Visions arise of a scene of mirth,
   And a ball-room belle that superbly poses—
A queenly woman of queenly worth,
And I am the happiest man on earth
   With a single flower from a bunch of roses.

111

Only her memory lives to-night—
 God in His wisdom her young life closes;
Over her grave may the turf be light,
Cover her coffin with roses white—
 She was always fond of the big white roses.

. . . . . .

Such are the visions that fade away—
 Man proposes and God disposes;
Look in the glass and I see to-day
Only an old man, worn and grey,
 Bending his head to a bunch of roses.

BLACK SWANS

As I lie at rest on a patch of clover
In the Western Park when the day is done,
I watch as the wild black swans fly over
With their phalanx turned to the sinking sun;
And I hear the clang of their leader crying
To a lagging mate in the rearward flying,
And they fade away in the darkness dying,
Where the stars are mustering one by one.

Oh! ye wild black swans, 'twere a world of wonder
For a while to join in your westward flight,
With the stars above and the dim earth under,
Through the cooling air of the glorious night.
As we swept along on our pinions winging,
We should catch the chime of a church-bell ringing,
Or the distant note of a torrent singing,
Or the far-off flash of a station light.

From the northern lakes with the reeds and rushes,
Where the hills are clothed with a purple haze,
Where the bell-birds chime and the songs of thrushes
Make music sweet in the jungle maze,
They will hold their course to the westward ever,
Till they reach the banks of the old grey river,
Where the waters wash, and the reed-beds quiver
In the burning heat of the summer days.

Oh ! ye strange wild birds, will ye bear a greeting
To the folk that live in that western land ?
Then for every sweep of your pinions beating,
Ye shall bear a wish to the sunburnt band,
To the stalwart men who are stoutly fighting
With the heat and drought and the dust-storm
　　　smiting,
Yet whose life somehow has a strange inviting,
When once to the work they have put their hand.

Facing it yet !　Oh, my friend stout-hearted,
What does it matter for rain or shine,
For the hopes deferred and the gain departed ?
Nothing could conquer that heart of thine.
And thy health and strength are beyond confessing
As the only joys that are worth possessing.

May the days to come be as rich in blessing
As the days we spent in the auld lang syne.

I would fain go back to the old grey river,
To the old bush days when our hearts were light,
But, alas ! those days they have fled for ever,
They are like the swans that have swept from sight.
And I know full well that the strangers' faces
Would meet us now in our dearest places ;
For our day is dead and has left no traces
But the thoughts that live in my mind to-night.

There are folk long dead, and our hearts would
        sicken—
We would grieve for them with a bitter pain,
If the past could live and the dead could quicken,
We then might turn to that life again.
But on lonely nights we would hear them calling,
We should hear their steps on the pathways falling,
We should loathe the life with a hate appalling
In our lonely rides by the ridge and plain.

                .   .   .   .   .   .

In the silent park is a scent of clover,
And the distant roar of the town is dead,

And I hear once more as the swans fly over
Their far-off clamour from overhead.
They are flying west, by their instinct guided,
And for man likewise is his fate decided,
And griefs apportioned and joys divided
By a mighty power with a purpose dread.

THE ALL RIGHT 'UN

He came from 'further out,'
That land of heat and drought
And dust and gravel.
He got a touch of sun,
And rested at the run
Until his cure was done,
And he could travel.

When spring had decked the plain,
He flitted off again
As flit the swallows.
And from that western land,
When many months were spanned,
A letter came to hand,
Which read as follows:

' Dear sir, I take my pen
' In hopes that all your men
' And you are hearty

117

THE ALL RIGHT 'UN

' You think that I've forgot
' Your kindness, Mr. Scott,
' Oh, no, dear sir, I'm not
' That sort of party.

' You sometimes bet, I know,
 Well, now you'll have a show
' The ' books ' to frighten.
' Up here at Wingadee
' Young Billy Fife and me
' We're training Strife, and he
' Is a all right 'un.

' Just now we're running byes,
' But, sir, first time he tries
' I'll send you word of.
' And running ' on the crook '
' Their measures we have took,
' It is the deadest hook
' You ever heard of.

' So when we lets him go,
' Why, then, I'll let you know,
' And you can have a show
' To put a mite on.

'Now, sir, my leave I'll take,
'Yours truly, William Blake.
'P.S.—Make no mistake,
'*He's a all right 'un.*'

.   .   .   .   .

By next week's *Riverine*
I saw my friend had been
A bit too cunning.
I read : ' The racehorse Strife
'And jockey William Fife
'Disqualified for life—
'Suspicious running.'

But though they spoilt his game,
I reckon all the same
I fairly ought to claim
My friend a white 'un.
For though he wasn't straight,
His deeds would indicate
His heart at any rate
Was ' a all right 'un.'

THE BOSS OF THE 'ADMIRAL LYNCH'

DID you ever hear tell of Chili? I was readin' the
    other day
Of President Balmaceda and of how he was sent away.
It seems that he didn't suit 'em—they thought that
    they'd like a change,
So they started an insurrection and chased him across
    the range.
They seemed to be restless people—and, judging by
    what you hear,
They raise up these revolutions 'bout two or three
    times a year;
And the man that goes out of office, he goes for the
    boundary *quick*,
For there isn't no vote by ballot—it's bullets that
    does the trick.
And it ain't like a real battle, where the prisoners'
    lives are spared,

And they fight till there's one side beaten and then
there's a truce declared,

And the man that has got the licking goes down like
a blooming lord
To hand in his resignation and give up his blooming
sword,
And the other man bows and takes it, and everything's
all polite —
This wasn't that kind of a picnic, this wasn't that sort
of a fight.
For the pris'ners they took—they shot 'em ; 'no odds
were they small or great,
If they'd collared old Balmaceda, they reckoned to
shoot him straight.
A lot of bloodthirsty devils they were—but there ain't
a doubt
They must have been real plucked 'uns—the way that
they fought it out,
And the king of 'em all, I reckon, the man that could
stand a pinch,
Was the boss of a one-horse gunboat.   They called
her the 'Admiral Lynch.'

Well, he was for Balmaceda, and after the war was
    done,
And Balmaceda was beaten and his troops had been
    forced to run,
The other man fetched his army and proceeded to do
    things brown,
He marched 'em into the fortress and took command
    of the town.
Cannon and guns and horses troopin' along the road,
Rumblin' over the bridges, and never a foeman showed
Till they came in sight of the harbour, and the very
    first thing they see
Was this mite of a one-horse gunboat a-lying against
    the quay,
And there as they watched they noticed a flutter of
    crimson rag,
And under their eyes he hoisted old Balmaceda's flag.
Well, I tell you it fairly knocked 'em—it just took
    away their breath,
For he must ha' known if they caught him, 'twas
    nothin' but sudden death.
An' he'd got no fire in his furnace, no chance to put
    out to sea,
So he stood by his gun and waited with his vessel
    against the quay.

Well, they sent him a civil message to say that the
    war was done,
And most of his side were corpses, and all that were
    left had run ;
And blood had been spilt sufficient, so they gave him
    a chance to decide
If he'd haul down his bit of bunting and come on the
    winning side.
He listened and heard their message, and answered
    them all polite,
That he was a Spanish hidalgo, and the men of his
    race *must* fight !
A gunboat against an army, and with never a chance
    to run,
And them with their hundred cannon and him with a
    single gun :
The odds were a trifle heavy -- but he wasn't the sort
    to flinch,
So he opened fire on the army, did the boss of the
    'Admiral Lynch.'

They pounded his boat to pieces, they silenced his
    single gun,
And captured the whole consignment, for none of 'em
    cared to run ;

And it don't say whether they shot him—it don't even
    give his name—
But whatever they did I'll wager that he went to his
    graveyard game.
I tell you those old hidalgos so stately and so polite,
They turn out the real Maginnis when it comes to an
    uphill fight.
There was General Alcantara, who died in the heaviest
    brunt,
And General Alzereca was killed in the battle's front;
But the king of 'em all, I reckon—the man that could
    stand a pinch—
Was the man who attacked the army with the gun-
    boat ' Admiral Lynch.'

A BUSHMAN'S SONG

I'M travellin' down the Castlereagh, and I'm a station
hand,
I'm handy with the ropin' pole, I'm handy with the
brand,
And I can ride a rowdy colt, or swing the axe all day,
But there's no demand for a station-hand along the
Castlereagh.

So it's shift, boys, shift, for there isn't the slightest
doubt
That we've got to make a shift to the stations further
out,
With the pack-horse runnin' after, for he follows like
a dog,
We must strike across the country at the old jig-jog.

This old black horse I'm riding—if you'll notice what's
his brand,

He wears the crooked R, you see—none better in the
    land.
He takes a lot of beatin', and the other day we tried,
For a bit of a joke, with a racing bloke, for twenty
    pounds a side.

It was shift, boys, shift, for there wasn't the slightest
    doubt
That I had to make him shift, for the money was
    nearly out ;
But he cantered home a winner, with the other one
    at the flog—
He's a red-hot sort to pick up with his old jig-jog.

I asked a cove for shearin' once along the Marthaguy
' We shear non-union here,' says he.   ' I call it scab,
    says I.
I looked along the shearin' floor before I turned to
    go—
There were eight or ten dashed Chinamen a-shearin
    in a row.

It was shift, boys, shift, for there wasn't the slightest
    doubt
It was time to make a shift with the leprosy about.

So I saddled up my horses, and I whistled to my dog,
And I left his scabby station at the old jig-jog.

I went to Illawarra, where my brother's got a farm,
He has to ask his landlord's leave before he lifts his
    arm ;
The landlord owns the country side—man, woman,
    dog, and cat,
They haven't the cheek to dare to speak without they
    touch their hat.

It was shift, boys, shift, for there wasn't the slightest
    doubt
Their little landlord god and I would soon have fallen
    out ;
Was I to touch my hat to him ?—was I his bloomin
    dog ?
So I makes for up the country at the old jig-jog.

But it's time that I was movin', I've a mighty way
    to go
Till I drink artesian water from a thousand feet below ;
Till I meet the overlanders with the cattle comin'
    down,
And I'll work a while till I make a pile, then have a
    spree in town.

A BUSHMAN'S SONG

So, it's shift, boys, shift, for there isn't the slightest
    doubt

We've got to make a shift to the stations further out ;

The pack-horse runs behind us, for he follows like a
    dog,

And we cross a lot of country at the old jig-jog.

HOW GILBERT DIED

THERE's never a stone at the sleeper's head,
  There's never a fence beside,
And the wandering stock on the grave may tread
  Unnoticed and undenied,
But the smallest child on the Watershed
  Can tell you how Gilbert died.

For he rode at dusk, with his comrade Dunn
  To the hut at the Stockman's Ford,
In the waning light of the sinking sun
  They peered with a fierce accord.
They were outlaws both—and on each man's head
  Was a thousand pounds reward.

They had taken toll of the country round,
  And the troopers came behind
With a black that tracked like a human hound
  In the scrub and the ranges blind :

He could run the trail where a white man's eye
    No sign of a track could find.

He had hunted them out of the One Tree Hill
    And over the Old Man Plain,
But they wheeled their tracks with a wild beast's skill,
    And they made for the range again.
Then away to the hut where their grandsire dwelt,
    They rode with a loosened rein.

And their grandsire gave them a greeting bold :
    ' Come in and rest in peace,
' No safer place does the country hold—
    ' With the night pursuit must cease,
' And we'll drink success to the roving boys,
    ' And to hell with the black police.'

But they went to death when they entered there,
    In the hut at the Stockman's Ford,
For their grandsire's words were as false as fair—
    They were doomed to the hangman's cord.
He had sold them both to the black police
    For the sake of the big reward.

In the depth of night there are forms that glide
    As stealthy as serpents creep,

And around the hut where the outlaws hide
   They plant in the shadows deep,
And they wait till the first faint flush of dawn
   Shall waken their prey from sleep.

But Gilbert wakes while the night is dark—
   A restless sleeper, aye,
He has heard the sound of a sheep-dog's bark,
   And his horse's warning neigh,
And he says to his mate, ' There are hawks abroad
   ' And it's time that we went away.'

Their rifles stood at the stretcher head,
   Their bridles lay to hand,
They wakened the old man out of his bed,
   When they heard the sharp command :
' In the name of the Queen lay down your arms,
   ' Now, Dunn and Gilbert, stand ! '

Then Gilbert reached for his rifle true
   That close at his hand he kept,
He pointed it straight at the voice and drew,
   But never a flash outleapt,
For the water ran from the rifle breech—
   It was drenched while the outlaws slept.

Then he dropped the piece with a bitter oath,
   And he turned to his comrade Dunn :
' We are sold,' he said, ' we are dead men both,
   ' But there may be a chance for one ;
' I'll stop and I'll fight with the pistol here,
   ' You take to your heels and run.'

So Dunn crept out on his hands and knees
   In the dim, half-dawning light,
And he made his way to a patch of trees,
   And vanished among the night,
And the trackers hunted his tracks all day,
   But they never could trace his flight.

But Gilbert walked from the open door
   In a confident style and rash ;
He heard at his side the rifles roar,
   And he heard the bullets crash.
But he laughed as he lifted his pistol-hand,
   And he fired at the rifle flash.

Then out of the shadows the troopers aimed
   At his voice and the pistol sound,

With the rifle flashes the darkness flamed,
    He staggered and spun around,
And they riddled his body with rifle balls
    As it lay on the blood-soaked ground.

There's never a stone at the sleeper's head,
    There's never a fence beside,
And the wandering stock on the grave may tread
    Unnoticed and undenied,
But the smallest child on the Watershed
    Can tell you how Gilbert died.

THE FLYING GANG

I SERVED my time, in the days gone by,
　　In the railway's clash and clang,
And I worked my way to the end, and I
　　Was the head of the ' Flying Gang.'
'Twas a chosen band that was kept at hand
　　In case of an urgent need,
Was it south or north we were started forth,
　　And away at our utmost speed.
　　　If word reached town that a bridge was down,
　　　　The imperious summons rang—
　　　' Come out with the pilot engine sharp,
　　　　And away with the flying gang.'

Then a piercing scream and a rush of steam
　　As the engine moved ahead,
With a measured beat by the slum and street
　　Of the busy town we fled,

By the uplands bright and the homesteads white,
  With the rush of the western gale,
And the pilot swayed with the pace we made
  As she rocked on the ringing rail.
    And the country children clapped their hands
      As the engine's echoes rang,
    But their elders said : ' There is work ahead
      When they send for the flying gang.'

Then across the miles of the saltbush plain
  That gleamed with the morning dew,
Where the grasses waved like the ripening grain
  The pilot engine flew,
A fiery rush in the open bush
  Where the grade marks seemed to fly,
And the order sped on the wires ahead,
  The pilot *must* go by.
    The Governor's special must stand aside,
      And the fast express go hang,
    Let your orders be that the line is free
      For the boys of the flying gang.

SHEARING AT CASTLEREAGH

THE bell is set a-ringing, and the engine gives a toot,
There's five and thirty shearers here are shearing for
    the loot,
So stir yourselves, you penners-up, and shove the
    sheep along,
The musterers are fetching them a hundred thousand
    strong,
And make your collie dogs speak up—what would
    the buyers say
In London if the wool was late this year from Castle-
    reagh ?

The man that ' rung ' the Tubbo shed is not the ringer
    here,
That stripling from the Cooma side can teach him
    how to shear.
They trim away the ragged locks, and rip the cutter
    goes,

And leaves a track of snowy fleece from brisket to
   the nose ;
It's lovely how they peel it off with never stop nor
   stay,
They're racing for the ringer's place this year at
   Castlereagh.

The man that keeps the cutters sharp is growling in
   his cage,
He's always in a hurry and he's always in a rage—
' You clumsy-fisted mutton-heads, you'd turn a fellow
   sick,
' You pass yourselves as shearers, you were born to
   swing a pick.
' Another broken cutter here, that's two you've broke
   to-day,
' It's awful how such crawlers come to shear at Castle-
   reagh.'

The youngsters picking up the fleece enjoy the merry
   din,
They throw the classer up the fleece, he throws it to
   the bin ;
The pressers standing by the rack are waiting for the
   wool,

There's room for just a couple more, the press is
    nearly full ;
Now jump upon the lever, lads, and heave and heave
    away,
Another bale of golden fleece is branded   Castlereagh.

THE WIND'S MESSAGE

THERE came a whisper down the Bland between the
    dawn and dark,
Above the tossing of the pines, above the river's flow;
It stirred the boughs of giant gums and stalwart
    ironbark;
It drifted where the wild ducks played amid the
    swamps below;
It brought a breath of mountain air from off the hills
    of pine,
A scent of eucalyptus trees in honey-laden bloom;
And drifting, drifting far away along the southern
    line
It caught from leaf and grass and fern a subtle strange
    perfume.

It reached the toiling city folk, but few there were
    that heard—
The rattle of their busy life had choked the whisper
    down;

And some but caught a fresh-blown breeze with scent
    of pine that stirred
A thought of blue hills far away beyond the smoky
    town ;
And others heard the whisper pass, but could not
    understand
The magic of the breeze's breath that set their hearts
    aglow,
Nor how the roving wind could bring across the Over-
    land
A sound of voices silent now and songs of long ago.

But some that heard the whisper clear were filled
    with vague unrest ;
The breeze had brought its message home, they could
    not fixed abide ;
Their fancies wandered all the day towards the blue
    hills' breast,
Towards the sunny slopes that lie along the riverside,
The mighty rolling western plains are very fair to see,
Where waving to the passing breeze the silver myalls
    stand,
But fairer are the giant hills, all rugged though they
    be,
From which the two great rivers rise that run along
    the Bland.

Oh! rocky range and rugged spur and river running
   clear,
That swings around the sudden bends with swirl of
   snow-white foam,
Though we, your sons, are far away, we sometimes
   seem to hear
The message that the breezes bring to call the
   wanderers home.
The mountain peaks are white with snow that feeds
   a thousand rills,
Along the river banks the maize grows tall on virgin
   land,
And we shall live to see once more those sunny
   southern hills,
And strike once more the bridle track that leads
   along the Bland.

JOHNSON'S ANTIDOTE

Down along the Snakebite River, where the over-
    landers camp,
Where the serpents are in millions, all of the most
    deadly stamp ;
Where the station-cook in terror, nearly every time
    he bakes,
Mixes up among the doughboys half-a-dozen poison-
    snakes :
Where the wily free-selector walks in armour-plated
    pants,
And defies the stings of scorpions, and the bites of
    bull-dog ants :
Where the adder and the viper tear each other by
    the throat,
There it was that William Johnson sought his snake-
    bite antidote.

Johnson was a free-selector, and his brain went rather
    queer,
For the constant sight of serpents filled him with a
    deadly fear;
So he tramped his free-selection, morning, afternoon,
    and night,
Seeking for some great specific that would cure the
    serpent's bite.
Till King Billy, of the Mooki, chieftain of the flour-
    bag head,
Told him, 'Spos'n snake bite pfeller, pfeller mostly
    drop down dead;
'Spos'n snake bite old goanna, then you watch a
    while you see,
'Old goanna cure himself with eating little pfeller
    tree.'
'That's the cure,' said William Johnson, 'point me
    out this plant sublime,'
But King Billy, feeling lazy, said he'd go another
    time.
Thus it came to pass that Johnson, having got the
    tale by rote,
Followed every stray goanna, seeking for the antidote.

Loafing once beside the river, while he thought his
    heart would break,
There he saw a big goanna fighting with a tiger-
    snake,
In and out they rolled and wriggled, bit each other,
    heart and soul,
Till the valiant old goanna swallowed his opponent
    whole.
Breathless, Johnson sat and watched him, saw him
    struggle up the bank,
Saw him nibbling at the branches of some bushes,
    green and rank ;
Saw him, happy and contented, lick his lips, as off he
    crept,
While the bulging in his stomach showed where his
    opponent slept.
Then a cheer of exultation burst aloud from Johnson's
    throat ;
' Luck at last,' said he, ' I've struck it ! 'tis the famous
    antidote.'

' Here it is, the Grand Elixir, greatest blessing ever
    known,
' Twenty thousand men in India die each year of
    snakes alone.

'Think of all the foreign nations, negro, chow, and
    blackamoor,
'Saved from sudden expiration, by my wondrous
    snakebite cure.
'It will bring me fame and fortune! In the happy
    days to be,
' Men of every clime and nation will be round to gaze
    on me—
' Scientific men in thousands, men of mark and men
    of note,
' Rushing down the Mooki River, after Johnson's
    antidote.
' It will cure *delirium tremens*, when the patient's eye-
    balls stare
' At imaginary spiders, snakes which really are not
    there.
' When he thinks he sees them wriggle, when he
    thinks he sees them bloat,
' It will cure him just to think of Johnson's Snakebite
    Antidote.'

Then he rushed to the museum, found a scientific
    man—
' Trot me out a deadly serpent, just the deadliest you
    can ;

' I intend to let him bite me, all the risk I will endure,
' Just to prove the sterling value of my wondrous
    snakebite cure.
' Even though an adder bit me, back to life again I'd
    float ;
'Snakes are out of date, I tell you, since I've found
    the antidote.'

Said the scientific person, 'If you really want to die,
' Go ahead—but, if you're doubtful, let your sheep-
    dog have a try.
' Get a pair of dogs and try it, let the snake give both
    a nip ;
'Give your dog the snakebite mixture, let the other
    fellow rip ;
' If he dies ard yours survives him, then it proves the
    thing is good.
' Will you fetch your dog and try it ?' Johnson rather
    thought he would.
So he went and fetched his canine, hauled him for-
    ward by the throat.
'Stump, old man,' says he, 'we'll show them we've
    the genwine antidote.'

Both the dogs were duly loaded with the poison-
gland's contents;
Johnson gave his dog the mixture, then sat down to
wait events.
'Mark,' he said, 'in twenty minutes Stump'll be a-
rushing round,
'While the other wretched creature lies a corpse upon
the ground.'
But, alas for William Johnson! ere they'd watched a
half-hour's spell
Stumpy was as dead as mutton, t'other dog was live
and well.
And the scientific person hurried off with utmost
speed,
Tested Johnson's drug and found it was a deadly
poison-weed;
Half a tumbler killed an emu, half a spoonful killed a
goat,
All the snakes on earth were harmless to that awful
antidote.

.   .   .   .   .   .

Down along the Mooki River, on the overlanders'
camp,

Where the serpents are in millions, all of the most
    deadly stamp,
Wanders, daily, William Johnson, down among those
    poisonous hordes,
Shooting every stray goanna, calls them 'black and
    yaller frauds.'
And King Billy, of the Mooki, cadging for the cast-
    off coat,
Somehow seems to dodge the subject of the snake-bite
    antidote.

AMBITION AND ART

AMBITION

I AM the maid of the lustrous eyes
   Of great fruition,
Whom the sons of men that are over-wise
   Have called Ambition.

And the world's success is the only goal
   I have within me ;
The meanest man with the smallest soul
   May woo and win me.

For the lust of power and the pride of place
   To all I proffer.
Wilt thou take thy part in the crowded race
   For what I offer ?

The choice is thine, and the world is wide—
   Thy path is lonely.
I may not lead and I may not guide—
   I urge thee only.

I am just a whip and a spur that smites
    To fierce endeavour.
In the restless days and the sleepless nights
    I urge thee ever.

Thou shalt wake from sleep with a startled cry,
    In fright upleaping
At a rival's step as it passes by
    Whilst thou art sleeping.

Honour and truth shall be overthrown
    In fierce desire ;
Thou shalt use thy friend as a stepping-stone
    To mount thee higher.

When the curtain falls on the sordid strife
    That seemed so splendid,
Thou shalt look with pain on the wasted life
    That thou hast ended.

Thou hast sold thy life for a guerdon small
    In fitful flashes ;
There has been reward—but the end of all
    Is dust and ashes.

For the night has come and it brings to naught
    Thy projects cherished,

And thine epitaph shall in brass be wrought—
   ' He lived and perished.'

ART

I wait for thee at the outer gate,
   My love, mine only ;
Wherefore tarriest thou so late
   While I am lonely.

Thou shalt seek my side with a footstep swift,
   In thee implanted
Is the love of Art and the greatest gift
   That God has granted.

And the world's concerns with its rights and wrongs
   Shall seem but small things—
Poet or painter, a singer of songs,
   Thine art is all things.

For the wine of life is a woman's love
   To keep beside thee ;
But the love of Art is a thing above—
   A star to guide thee.

As the years go by with thy love of Art
  All undiminished,
Thou shalt end thy days with a quiet heart—
  Thy work is finished.

So the painter fashions a picture strong
  That fadeth never,
And the singer singeth a wond'rous song
  That lives for ever.

THE DAYLIGHT IS DYING

The daylight is dying
    Away in the west,
The wild birds are flying
    In silence to rest ;
In leafage and frondage
    Where shadows are deep,
They pass to its bondage—
    The kingdom of sleep.
And watched in their sleeping
    By stars in the height,
They rest in your keeping,
    Oh, wonderful night.

When night doth her glories
    Of starshine unfold,
'Tis then that the stories
    Of bush-land are told.
Unnumbered I hold them
    In memories bright,
But who could unfold them,
    Or read them aright ?

153

Beyond all denials
   The stars in their glories
The breeze in the myalls
   Are part of these stories.
The waving of grasses,
   The song of the river
That sings as it passes
   For ever and ever,
The hobble-chains' rattle,
   The calling of birds,
The lowing of cattle
   Must blend with the words.
Without these, indeed, you
   Would find it ere long,
As though I should read you
   The words of a song
That lamely would linger
   When lacking the rune,
The voice of the singer,
   The lilt of the tune.

But, as one half-hearing
   An old-time refrain,
With memory clearing,
   Recalls it again,

These tales, roughly wrought of
  The bush and its ways,
May call back a thought of
  The wandering days,
And, blending with each
  In the mem ries that throng,
There haply shall reach
  You some echo of song.

IN DEFENCE OF THE BUSH

So you're back from up the country, Mister Towns-
    man, where you went,
And you're cursing all the business in a bitter discon-
    tent ;
Well, we grieve to disappoint you, and it makes us
    sad to hear
That it wasn't cool and shady—and there wasn't
    plenty beer,
And the loony bullock snorted when you first came
    into view ;
Well, you know it's not so often that he sees a swell
    like you ;
And the roads were hot and dusty, and the plains
    were burnt and brown,
And no doubt you're better suited drinking lemon
    squash in town.

Yet, perchance, if you should journey down the very
    track you went
In a month or two at furthest you would wonder
    what it meant,
Where the sunbaked earth was gasping like a creature
    in its pain
You would find the grasses waving like a field of
    summer grain,
And the miles of thirsty gutters blocked with sand
    and choked with mud,
You would find them mighty rivers with a turbid,
    sweeping flood ;
For the rain and drought and sunshine make no
    changes in the street,
In the sullen line of buildings and the ceaseless tramp
    of feet ;
But the bush hath moods and changes, as the seasons
    rise and fall,
And the men who know the bush-land—they are loyal
    through it all.

    .   .   .   .   .   .

But you found the bush was dismal and a land of no
    delight,
Did you chance to hear a chorus in the shearers' huts
    at night ?

Did they ' rise up, William Riley ' by the camp-fire's
    cheery blaze ?
Did they rise him as we rose him in the good old
    droving days ?
And the women of the homesteads and the men you
    chanced to meet—
Were their faces sour and saddened like the ' faces
    in the street,'
And the ' shy selector children '—were they better
    now or worse
Than the little city urchins who would greet you with
    a curse ?
Is not such a life much better than the squalid street
    and square
Where the fallen women flaunt it in the fierce electric
    glare,
Where the sempstress plies her sewing till her eyes
    are sore and red
In a filthy, dirty attic toiling on for daily bread ?
Did you hear no sweeter voices in the music of the
    bush
Than the roar of trams and 'buses, and the war-
    whoop of ' the push ? '
Did the magpies rouse your slumbers with their carol
    sweet and strange ?

Did you hear the silver chiming of the bell-birds on
 the range?
But, perchance, the wild birds' music by your senses
 was despised,
For you say you'll stay in townships till the bush is
 civilised.
Would you make it a tea-garden and on Sundays
 have a band
Where the ' blokes ' might take their ' donahs,' with a
 public ' close at hand?
You had better stick to Sydney and make merry with
 the ' push,'
For the bush will never suit you, and you'll never
 suit the bush.

LAST WEEK

OH, the new-chum went to the back block run,
But he should have gone there last week.
He tramped ten miles with a loaded gun,
But of turkey or duck he saw never a one,
For he should have been there last week,
  They said,
There were flocks of 'em there last week.

He wended his way to a waterfall,
And he should have gone there last week.
He carried a camera, legs and all,
But the day was hot, and the stream was small,
For he should have gone there last week,
  They said.
They drowned a man there last week.

He went for a drive, and he made a start,
Which should have been made last week,
For the old horse died of a broken heart;

160

So he footed it home and he dragged the cart—
But the horse was all right last week,
   They said.
He trotted a match last week.

So he asked the bushies who came from far
To visit the town last week,
If they'd dine with him, and they said ' Hurrah !
But there wasn't a drop in the whisky jar—
You should have been here last week,
   He said,
I drank it all up last week !

THOSE NAMES

THE shearers sat in the firelight, hearty and hale and
    strong,
After the hard day's shearing, passing the joke along :
The 'ringer' that shore a hundred, as they never
    were shorn before,
And the novice who, toiling bravely, had tommy-
    hawked half a score,
The tarboy, the cook, and the slushy, the sweeper
    that swept the board,
The picker-up, and the penner, with the rest of the
    shearing horde.
There were men from the inland stations where the
    skies like a furnace glow,
And men from the Snowy River, the land of the frozen
    snow ;
There were swarthy Queensland drovers who reck-
    oned all land by miles,

162

And farmers' sons from the Murray, where many a
    vineyard smiles.
They started at telling stories when they wearied of
    cards and games,
And to give these stories a flavour they threw in some
    local names,
And a man from the bleak Monaro, away on the
    tableland,
He fixed his eyes on the ceiling, and he started to
    play his hand.

He told them of Adjintoothbong, where the pine-clad
    mountains freeze,
And the weight of the snow in summer breaks
    branches off the trees,
And, as he warmed to the business, he let them have
    it strong—
Nimitybelle, Conargo, Wheeo, Bongongolong ;
He lingered over them fondly, because they recalled
    to mind
A thought of the old bush homestead, and the girl
    that he left behind.
Then the shearers all sat silent till a man in the
    corner rose ;
Said he, ' I've travelled a-plenty but never heard
    names like those.

' Out in the western districts, out on the Castlereagh
' Most of the names are easy—short for a man to say.

' You've heard of Mungrybambone and the Gunda-
        bluey pine,
' Quobbotha, Girilambone, and Terramungamine,
' Quambone, Eunonyhareenyha, Wee Waa, and
        Buntijo—'
But the rest of the shearers stopped him : ' For the
        sake of your jaw, go slow,
' If you reckon those names are short ones out where
        such names prevail,
' Just try and remember some long ones before you
        begin the tale.'
And the man from the western district, though never
        a word he said,
Just winked with his dexter eyelid, and then he
        retired to bed.

A BUSH CHRISTENING

On the outer Barcoo where the churches are few,
    And men of religion are scanty,
On a road never cross'd 'cept by folk that are lost,
    One Michael Magee had a shanty.

Now this Mike was the dad of a ten year old lad,
    Plump, healthy, and stoutly conditioned;
He was strong as the best, but poor Mike had no rest
    For the youngster had never been christened.

And his wife used to cry, ' If the darlin' should die
    ' Saint Peter would not recognise him.'
But by luck he survived till a preacher arrived,
    Who agreed straightaway to baptise him.

Now the artful young rogue, while they held their
    collogue,
    With his ear to the keyhole was listenin',

And he muttered in fright, while his features turned
    white,
   ' What the divil and all is this christenin'?'

He was none of your dolts, he had seen them brand
    colts,
   And it seemed to his small understanding,
If the man in the frock made him one of the flock,
   It must mean something very like branding.

So away with a rush he set off for the bush,
   While the tears in his eyelids they glistened—
' 'Tis outrageous,' says he, ' to brand youngsters like
    me,
   ' I'll be dashed if I'll stop to be christened!'

Like a young native dog he ran into a log,
   And his father with language uncivil,
Never heeding the ' praste ' cried aloud in his haste,
   ' Come out and be christened, you divil!'

But he lay there as snug as a bug in a rug,
   And his parents in vain might reprove him,
Till his reverence spoke (he was fond of a joke)
   ' I've a notion,' says he, ' that'll move him.'

' Poke a stick up the log, give the spalpeen a prog ;
 ' Poke him aisy—don't hurt him or maim him,
' 'Tis not long that he'll stand, I've the water at hand,
 ' As he rushes out this end I'll name him.

' Here he comes, and for shame ! ye've forgotten the
   name—
 ' Is it Patsy or Michael or Dinnis ? '
Here the youngster ran out, and the priest gave a
   shout—
 ' Take your chance, anyhow, wid ' Maginnis ' ! '

As the howling young cub ran away to the scrub
 Where he knew that pursuit would be risky,
The priest, as he fled, flung a flask at his head
 That was labelled ' MAGINNIS'S WHISKY ! '

And Maginnis Magee has been made a J.P.,
 And the one thing he hates more than sin is
To be asked by the folk, who have heard of the joke,
 How he came to be christened ' Maginnis ' !

HOW THE FAVOURITE BEAT US

' AYE,' said the boozer, ' I tell you it's true, sir,
' I once was a punter with plenty of pelf,
' But gone is my glory, I'll tell you the story
' How I stiffened my horse and got stiffened myself.

' 'Twas a mare called the Cracker, I came down to
    back her,
' But found she was favourite all of a rush,
' The folk just did pour on to lay six to four on,
' And several bookies were killed in the crush.

' It seems old Tomato was stiff, though a starter ;
' They reckoned him fit for the Caulfield to keep.
' The Bloke and the Donah were scratched by their
    owner,
' He only was offered three-fourths of the sweep.

' We knew Salamander was slow as a gander,
' The mare could have beat him the length of the
    straight,

'And old Manumission was out of condition,
'And most of the others were running off weight.

'No doubt someone 'blew it,' for everyone knew it,
'The bets were all gone, and I muttered in spite
'If I can't get a copper, by Jingo, I'll stop her,
'Let the public fall in, it will serve the brutes right.'

I said to the jockey, 'Now, listen, my cocky,
You watch as you're cantering down by the stand,
'I'll wait where that toff is and give you the office,
'You're only to win if I lift up my hand.'

'I then tried to back her—'What price is the
          Cracker?'
'Our books are all full, sir,' each bookie did swear;
'My mind, then, I made up, my fortune I played up
'I bet every shilling against my own mare.

'I strolled to the gateway, the mare in the straight-
          way
'Was shifting and dancing, and pawing the ground,
'The boy saw me enter and wheeled for his canter,
'When a darned great mosquito came buzzing around.

'They breed 'em at Hexham, it's risky to vex 'em,
'They suck a man dry at a sitting, no doubt,
'But just as the mare passed, he fluttered my hair
    past,
'I lifted my hand, and I flattened him out.

'I was stunned when they started, the mare simply
    darted
'Away to the front when the flag was let fall,
'For none there could match her, and none tried to
    catch her—
'She finished a furlong in front of them all.

'You bet that I went for the boy, whom I sent for
'The moment he weighed and came out of the stand—
'Who paid you to win it? Come, own up this minute.'
'Lord love yer,' said he, 'why you lifted your hand.'

''Twas true, by St. Peter, that cursed 'muskeeter'
'Had broke me so broke that I hadn't a brown,
'And you'll find the best course is when dealing with
    horses
  To win when you're able, and *keep your hands down.*

THE GREAT CALAMITY

MacFierce'un came to Whiskeyhurst
  When summer days were hot,
And bided there wi' Jock McThirst,
  A brawny brother Scot.
Gude Faith ! They made the whisky fly,
  Like Highland chieftains true,
And when they'd drunk the beaker dry
  They sang ' We are nae fou ! '

    ' There is nae folk like oor ain folk,
      ' Sae gallant and sae true.'
    They sang the only Scottish joke
      Which is, ' We are nae fou.'

Said bold McThirst, ' Let Saxons jaw
  ' Aboot their great concerns,
' But bonny Scotland beats them a',
  ' The land o' cakes and Burns,

171

'The land o' partridge, deer, and grouse,
  'Fill up your glass, I beg,
'There's muckle whusky i' the house,
  'Forbye what's in the keg.'

    And here a hearty laugh he laughed,
      'Just come wi' me, I beg.'
    MacFierce'un saw with pleasure daft
      A fifty-gallon keg.

'Losh, man, that's grand,' MacFierce'un cried,
  'Saw ever man the like,
Now, wi' the daylight, I maun ride
  'To meet a Southron tyke,
'But I'll be back ere summer's gone,
  'So bide for me, I beg,
'We'll make a grand assault upon
  'Yon deevil of a keg.'

   .   .   .   .   .   .

MacFierce'un rode to Whiskeyhurst,
  When summer days were gone,
And there he met with Jock McThirst
  Was greetin' all alone.
'McThirst what gars ye look sae blank ?
  'Have all yer wits gane daft ?

' Has that accursed Southron bank
  ' Called up your overdraft ?
' Is all your grass burnt up wi' drouth ?
  ' Is wool and hides gone flat ? '
McThirst replied, ' Gude friend, in truth,
  ' 'Tis muckle waur than that.'

' Has sair misfortune cursed your life
  ' That you should weep sae free ?
' Is harm upon your bonny wife,
  ' The children at your knee ?
' Is scaith upon your house and hame ? '
  McThirst upraised his head :
' My bairns hae done the deed of shame—
  ' 'Twere better they were dead.

' To think my bonny infant son
  ' Should do the deed o' guilt—
' *He let the whuskey spigot run,*
  ' *And a' the whuskey's spilt ?* '

   .   .   .   .   .   .

Upon them both these words did bring
  A solemn silence deep,
Gude faith, it is a fearsome thing
  To see two strong men weep.

COME-BY-CHANCE

As I pondered very weary o'er a volume long and
  dreary—
For the plot was void of interest—'twas the Postal
  Guide, in fact,
There I learnt the true location, distance, size, and
  population
Of each township, town, and village in the radius of
  the Act.

And I learnt that Puckawidgee stands beside the
  Murrumbidgee,
And that Booleroi and Bumble get their letters twice
  a year,
Also that the post inspector, when he visited Collector,
Closed the office up instanter, and re-opened Dunga-
  lear.
174

But my languid mood forsook me, when I found a
    name that took me,
Quite by chance I came across it—' Come-by-Chance
    was what I read ;
No location was assigned it, not a thing to help one
    find it,
Just an N which stood for northward, and the rest
    was all unsaid.

I shall leave my home, and forthward wander stoutly
    to the northward
Till I come by chance across it, and I'll straightway
    settle down,
For there can't be any hurry, nor the slightest cause
    for worry
Where the telegraph don't reach you nor the railways
    run to town.

And one's letters and exchanges come by chance
    across the ranges,
Where a wiry young Australian leads a pack-horse
    once a week,
And the good news grows by keeping, and you're
    spared the pain of weeping
Over bad news when the mailman drops the letters in
    the creek.

But I fear, and more's the pity, that there's really no
such city,

For there's not a man can find it of the shrewdest
folk I know,

' Come-by-chance,' be sure it never means a land of
fierce endeavour,

It is just the careless country where the dreamers
only go.
.   .   .   .   .   .

Though we work and toil and hustle in our life of
haste and bustle,

All that makes our life worth living comes unstriven
for and free ;

Man may weary and importune, but the fickle goddess
Fortune

Deals him out his pain or pleasure, careless what his
worth may be.

All the happy times entrancing, days of sport and
nights of dancing,

Moonlit rides and stolen kisses, pouting lips and
loving glance :

When you think of these be certain you have looked
behind the curtain,

You have had the luck to linger just a while in
' Come-by-chance.'

UNDER THE SHADOW OF KILEY'S HILL

THIS is the place where they all were bred;
  Some of the rafters are standing still;
Now they are scattered and lost and dead,
Every one from the old nest fled,
  Out of the shadow of Kiley's Hill.

Better it is that they ne'er came back—
  Changes and chances are quickly rung;
Now the old homestead is gone to rack,
Green is the grass on the well-worn track
  Down by the gate where the roses clung.

Gone is the garden they kept with care;
  Left to decay at its own sweet will,
Fruit trees and flower beds eaten bare,
Cattle and sheep where the roses were,
  Under the shadow of Kiley's Hill.

177

Where are the children that throve and grew
  In the old homestead in days gone by?
One is away on the far Barcoo
Watching his cattle the long year through,
  Watching them starve in the droughts and die

One in the town where all cares are rife,
  Weary with troubles that cramp and kill,
Fain would be done with the restless strife,
Fain would go back to the old bush life,
  Back to the shadow of Kiley's Hill.

One is away on the roving quest,
  Seeking his share of the golden spoil,
Out in the wastes of the trackless west,
Wandering ever he gives the best
  Of his years and strength to the hopeless toil.

What of the parents? That unkept mound
  Shows where they slumber united still;
Rough is their grave, but they sleep as sound
Out on the range as on holy ground,
  Under the shadow of Kiley's Hill.

JIM CAREW

Born of a thoroughbred English race,
  Well proportioned and closely knit,
Neat of figure and handsome face,
  Always ready and always fit,
Hard and wiry of limb and thew,
That was the ne'er-do-well Jim Carew.

One of the sons of the good old land—
  Many a year since his like was known;
Never a game but he took command,
  Never a sport but he held his own;
Gained at his college a triple blue—
Good as they make them was Jim Carew.

Came to grief—was it card or horse?
  Nobody asked and nobody cared;

Ship him away to the bush of course,
   Ne'er-do-well fellows are easily spared ;
Only of women a tolerable few
Sorrowed at parting with Jim Carew.

Gentleman Jim on the cattle camp,
   Sitting his horse with an easy grace ;
But the reckless living has left its stamp
   In the deep drawn lines of that handsome face,
And a harder look in those eyes of blue :
Prompt at a quarrel is Jim Carew.

Billy the Lasher was out for gore—
   Twelve-stone navvy with chest of hair,
When he opened out with a hungry roar
   On a ten-stone man it was hardly fair ;
But his wife was wise if his face she knew
By the time you were done with him, Jim Carew.

Gentleman Jim in the stockmen's hut
   Works with them, toils with them, side by side ;
As to his past—well, his lips are shut,
   'Gentleman once,' say his mates with pride ;
And the wildest Cornstalk can ne'er outdo
In feats of recklessness, Jim Carew.

What should he live for? A dull despair!
  Drink is his master and drags him down,
Water of Lethe that drowns all care.

  Gentleman Jim has a lot to drown,
And he reigns as king with a drunken crew,
Sinking to misery, Jim Carew.

Such is the end of the ne'er-do-well—
  Jimmy the Boozer, all down at heel;
But he straightens up when he's asked to tell
  His name and race, and a flash of steel
Still lightens up in those eyes of blue—
' I am, or—no, I *was*—Jim Carew.'

THE SWAGMAN'S REST

We buried old Bob where the bloodwoods wave
  At the foot of the Eaglehawk ;
We fashioned a cross on the old man's grave,
  For fear that his ghost might walk ;
We carved his name on a bloodwood tree,
  With the date of his sad decease,
And in place of ' Died from effects of spree,'
  We wrote ' May he rest in peace.'

For Bob was known on the Overland,
  A regular old bush wag,
Tramping along in the dust and sand,
  Humping his well-worn swag.
He would camp for days in the river-bed,
  And loiter and ' fish for whales.'
I'm into the swagman's yard,' he said,
  ' And I never shall find the rails.'

But he found the rails on that summer night
  For a better place—or worse,
As we watched by turns in the flickering light
  With an old black gin for nurse.
The breeze came in with the scent of pine,
  The river sounded clear,
When a change came on, and we saw the sign
  That told us the end was near.

But he spoke in a cultured voice and low—
  'I fancy they've "sent the route;"
'I once was an army man, you know,
  'Though now I'm a drunken brute;
'But bury me out where the bloodwoods wave,
  'And if ever you're fairly stuck,
'Just take and shovel me out of the grave
  'And, maybe, I'll bring you luck.

'For I've always heard—' here his voice fell weak,
  His strength was well-nigh sped,
He gasped and struggled and tried to speak,
  Then fell in a moment—dead.
Thus ended a wasted life and hard,
  Of energies misapplied—
Old Bob was out of the 'swagman's yard'
  And over the Great Divide.

The drought came down on the field and flock,
    And never a raindrop fell,
Though the tortured moans of the starving stock
    Might soften a fiend from hell.
And we thought of the hint that the swagman gave
    When he went to the Great Unseen—
We shovelled the skeleton out of the grave
    To see what his hint might mean.

We dug where the cross and the grave posts were,
    We shovelled away the mould,
When sudden a vein of quartz lay bare
    All gleaming with yellow gold.
'Twas a reef with never a fault nor baulk
    That ran from the range's crest,
And the richest mine on the Eaglehawk
    Is known as ' The Swagman's Rest.'

Bloxham & Chambers, Printers, Wentworth Place, Sydney.